Beckett's Children

Beckett's Children

A Literary Memoir

Michael Coffey

Evergreen Review Books

Beckett's Children: A Literary Memoir © 2024 Michael Coffey

Published by Evergreen Review Books, an imprint of OR Books

Visit our website at www.evergreenreview.com

All rights information: rights@orbooks.com

First printing 2024

Cataloging-in-Publication data is available from the Library of Congress.
A catalog record for this book is available from the British Library.

hardback ISBN 978-1-68219-608-3

JACKET FRONT: Debra Pearlman, *Seen Unseen III*, 2022. © Debra Pearlman.
Monotype (30 × 22 inches). Reproduced by permission of the artist.

Text and jacket design and typesetting by Laura Lindgren

The absent center is the ghost of a king.
—Susan Howe, *The Nonconformist's Memorial*

. . . in the silence you don't know . . .
—Samuel Beckett, *The Unnamable*

Ah well we pick up the stones we want.
And carry them forever.
—Joshua Coffey

PART I
The Leaves

Go, said the bird, for the leaves were full of children.
—T. S. Eliot, "Burnt Norton"

I've been looking in the leaves and listening in the leaves since I came of age, looking and listening for traces, voices, ghosts of lost birth parents, lost siblings or half siblings, for an extrusion of a family wholly out of sight, earshot, mind; extrusions into the fabric of the visible and the heard, I mean read on printed pages.

All the dead voices—are they dead?—a noise like wings, no like leaves, no like sand, no like leaves, they whisper they rustle they murmur. They rustle. They talk about their lives, says Vladimir. They may be dead—are they dead?—and still they have to talk about it. Do we listen?

Leaves, ashes.

Go, said the bird.

The way is fair for the wayfarer, I know—it is inscribed in the word, sort of. Lucky to catch a lift on a haywain, then—look at Bosch! The wains! Beckett talks about the wains, or rather the narrator of "First Love" does, a story, written in

French in the 1940s, unreleased till the 1970s, in both French and English, the author having for decades deemed it too personal. The narrator looks in vain for the wains after he leaves his love, his first love, Lulu, after the unexpected birth of a child. The wains! The wains! We see them as the dippers Big and Little, as if from a cistern or better yet a bucket, not wagons in the sky, major and minor, but let them come for me. Close enough the morphology if not the etymology.

Let's do the weather then here and now, and as always I will try to catch up to the here and now. I'll start with color, white where white is, downslope and trees, the birches, far below, a lake. Must be winter where I am from, or late, late fall. From where I sit, more the promise of a lake than a sighting hides below—none of the lake views that thrill the insurgent newcomers. We are old, aren't we. Gray the sky, vaulting down in sympathy with the slope—what's the phrase for a limb riding on another's limb? A kind of sistering, as timbers are sistered? Some stage direction perhaps? The road outside my window, my picture window, soot black the pavement, the black of black maples that form a kind of allée, and the pale green on the trunks, lichen I think, or moss, and the branchwork bare and straining now for the sky to notice, the sky which is falling now amidst strophes of bruised light.

Yes to sistering.

Language, I am trying to say, as a lifeline, hand over hand, this line you grab and pull hand over hand, you follow it in the dark, here's the dark, for dear life, it must end somewhere but its linearity is all the sense we have so follow it, hand over hand, it has its intricacies, its braided strength, like a rope and we move along it, I, we, you, whoever, it is sinuous, I'll grant that, we move around corners, uphill and downhill, a way, following the lifeline of language.

○ ○ ○ ○ ○

As if:

Not him . . . not then . . . so he said . . . he said to me . . . on the phone, yes . . . in the crackle . . . Krak Krak he said on a phone . . . it came to me . . . the telephone . . . out of the cradle . . . the cradle! . . . phone in my hand he said, Hello you it is Me, I'm not, no. Cheers, love . . . Ta . . . It's not me, he said to me. . . . So it's not him. . . . Do I care? . . . Yes. . . . Should I care? . . . Yes . . . but no, I don't know. . . . This is the thing: I don't care. . . . Yes, yes I do. . . . Ta, love! . . . Ha! It's not me, then, he said, not for me of him to me with me on me in me or by me . . . that's for him, not for me, to say. . . . For him not me! He's not buying . . . is SHE buying? . . . not him not here not now not then not me. . . . She? Didn't she say not then or did she say . . . not then now?—Not him . . . She! . . . Now now now stop that! . . . No, not now, not ever . . . not now not even . . . nohow, maybe . . . Ha! Never now but later, not early, early-ER! . . . I will check later . . . with her . . . no I won't. . . . I will NOT! . . . Not with her nor she nor him nor her . . . with me!. . . . He didn't say, did he (he did not say), but he said something, he said it was not true what I had said . . . what had I said? . . . What I had said, I will check . . . I'm the one for checking . . . checking this, ticking that. . . . I didn't say

anything was true . . . no, no. . . . I hide I hide, I said . . . I said,
is it you, I said . . . is it you, I said, and if it is you what did that
do . . . what did that say or do to what was said or unsaid . . .
by you . . . what did that do, to you, if it was you . . . but he said,
Not me . . . no way . . . don't hide, he said don't hide. It's sinking
in now. . . . He had the proof . . . No, she had the proof . . . no she
had the math! . . . Or the word . . . only a word . . . Now? Then he
said, did he say? To whom? . . . Not here, he said not here, I said,
not now? . . . Ha! Why not now? No I thought, it did not say it,
what is it, why not now, shook my head shook his head (if I could
have seen him) and I asked (if I could be heard), Not then? . . .
Not now? Ha! He wouldn't say when, I could hear him . . .
then . . . we used to say, back then, "Say when!" . . . we'd say
"when" when we meant now. Not now! Not then! I whisper . . .
"when."

Never even, what did it do to me. Not ever.

Where was I then? . . . I'd asked nicely . . . I took my time. . . . Not
right away, no . . . not right away . . . but over time, I took my
time . . . I took a lifetime . . . I did my reading . . . I read it all . . .
I read from start to go . . . I wrote, I scribbled, we all scribbled,
all we all we do. . . . It is lost. . . . No I don't read, no . . . don't
read Him Her Me She It! Nor he me Buster Keaton! Not then no
not now. . . . He would know now, gone now. . . . He would know
in many languages. . . . Babel, yes, the tower at Babel, yes. . . .
Gone now. . . . Behold the people . . . all one language. . . . Then
the dust, the rubble, gone now . . . all the myths, the noise . . . the
blood it spills . . . take that! . . . Like there was ever just one . . .
one language, one love . . . one . . . settling. . . . Unsettling! Keats
his swallows Yeats his swallows, dusk dusk . . . such lingo! . . .

*Such a songster! I can feel it coming . . . such a . . . poet! . . . In the
dead of night . . . in the dead of the blood . . . it is coming in the
dead of it all . . . and about time. . . . I wish it were him . . . no,
not him . . . but Him! . . . I wish it were a she . . . a Her! I wish it
were a she where he is . . . where I am. . . . Do I wish a she and he
and which he, and if so, why do I wish? . . . What does it mean,
he, she, it? . . . I wish them well, of course . . . I wish them all the
happiness . . . why not . . . if wishes were—what of it! . . . And so
on. . . . And so. . . . I wish them happiness . . . of him, of her, the
of, the happiness of she, of he . . . truth be told: she as his and he
as hers . . . them as mine . . . as me!*

*But he said no. . . . So it is no. She said no. . . . So a no a no. A
no to know. Not him, he said. . . . Not him, she said. . . . He can't
say, now, again, can he? . . . she can say, now, she can say she can
say all she wants, since he can't say now, again . . . no he can't,
he's dead . . . no longer . . . quick! . . . Still, still at last, as he
wished. I do not believe it! . . . She can say all she wants . . . yes,
okay, yes, she doesn't say, does not declaim, hers is silence too,
now hers is work too, so she says, hers is long, longer still still
long, still still . . . so she says, older I daresay, wiser I say . . . she
doesn't say now. . . . Or then . . . only I asked, I don't ask, now,
any more, over now think of over over . . . think of She of her or
He of him . . . what of Me? . . . be frank . . . what of Me! What of
the others, where are the others . . . not at all like the others, the
other sops, the saps, who whisper, the whisperers . . . I can't hear
them . . . not here not now . . . I go . . . it has happened. . . . It
has happened to me . . . to Me! Not Him! Not Her . . . none of the
Himselfs . . . not me, no not me . . . never me, and now me, but
not me that whispers—me that says.*

With the haloes of her breasts already darkening, Lulu hears from her lover, "Abort, abort."

As if not.

○ ○ ○ ○ ○

I would turn sixty in a couple of days. My wife suggested I do something for myself around my birthday, not in lieu of a nice dinner, as was our custom, but as something extra. So I ventured uptown on a bright, cold Sunday morning to the 92nd St. Y. The 11 a.m. event—with bagels and coffee— featured two of the editors of *The Letters of Samuel Beckett*, Martha Dow Fehsenfeld and Lois More Overbeck.

I owned all three of the volumes thus far published—there would be a fourth in two years' time. I had even reviewed the inaugural volume for *Publishers Weekly*. I had been reading Beckett since my junior year of college, spent in Dublin, but in the last four or five years I had been reading him more intensely, not yet exclusively, but with a scholarly focus I humored myself to think was unique.

I was among the youngest in attendance that morning, surrounded by those my seniors, mostly women. One who sat near me insisted I take the seat next to her, which she patted with her hand, telling me, "you're sitting here," and who wore a crooked ginger-colored wig and a layer of makeup between pink and orange, who four times asked me my name, and then where was I born, and then proudly declared that she, too, was a New Yorker by birth, born in "the only borough connected to the mainland of the United States: the Bronx. The rest are just islands, you know." All of these YMCA patrons arrived early to this 11 a.m. event, even the speakers—so the room sat still at near capacity for twenty minutes before things commenced, but which allowed me to take a good look around. In front of me sat a tiny, elegant, very thin woman, bent over quite a bit like a shepherd's crook, her hair a kind of gray-purple, done just so. She sat with her mouth open and one ear cocked trying to listen as people came by to make a fuss. She was Judith Schmidt, I was able to glean, who had worked at Grove Press and with whom, a bit later, in front of all, I would discuss at some volume her accompanying Mr. Beckett around town on his only visit to New York during the making of *Film* with Buster Keaton in 1964. She drove Grove editor Richard Seaver and Beckett to a ballpark to see baseball's two worst teams match wits for a doubleheader. In recounting the event, Judith said that Beckett was "a lovely, lovely, lovely man." She said baseball like "base-bool" and man like "me-ann." I was very happy to have met Judith Schmidt Douw, who would live only a few months more.

Marty and Lois were introduced by the director of programming at the Y. The two women stood at separate podiums in a modest-sized room with fifty or so people in folding chairs. There was some recounting of this enormous project now coming to fruition. Marty or Lois explained how Beckett kept no letters received nor carbons of letters sent. Each letter or postcard had to be located, recipient by recipient, and in the case of the many handwritten ones, Beckett's nearly indecipherable handwriting had to be transcribed, whether from French or English. Someone asked a question: was Beckett left-handed or right-handed? These women, who have been editing the letters for decades, did not know. I was surprised. I piped up that his right hand had developed an arthritic condition as he aged and I had read that his handwriting was not good as a result, so he must have been right-handed. Lois countered, sort of, that his handwriting was never good, so that was inconclusive. Marty said that after she'd first shaken Beckett's hand, she said to his close Dublin friend Con Leventhal, "Odd, but he held a pencil in his hand." And Con told her that was just the finger. Lois gave the name for the condition: Dupuytren's contracture, sometimes known as "the Celtic hand." I asked her to spell it; she did.

I did not ask any questions in the Q&A, though I did answer one. Someone asked, when did Beckett die, and the editors momentarily drew a blank and I piped up, "Twenty-five years ago, 1989." At the end, I did approach Lois Overbeck at the podium, with congratulations and sincere expressions of admiration for the scholarship and care in bringing the letters to light, and asked my question, the question I thought at the heart of my singular scholarly interest in an unexplored area of the Beckett life. "No, no," said Lois. "Do the math." I'd heard that before, but I had done the math, and I did not think that the math—that is, the calendar of days and the period of human gestation—ruled out the possibility that Beckett had fathered a daughter, who was alive and living in Connecticut and a poet.

An hour or so later I was on my own, walking in the very different air and light of the Upper East Side, brighter, more elevated, and more spacious than what I had become accustomed to in my decades living in the West Village and then farther downtown. Very different yet familiar. In fact, powerfully so.

I decided to stroll right past the 86th Street subway entrance, which I once knew so well, and instead stay in the sun and navigate the wide, blonde sidewalks toward my first neighborhood in New York, which was indeed on this Upper East Side, known as Yorkville then, and Germantown, then, who knows what now.

Where there once was a big Gimbel's department store, a movie house, a series of butchers and bakeries and hardware stores and bars now there were bank branches and fancy household furnishing joints and fashion outlets. When I turned south down Second Avenue at 86th Street I saw evidence of what I had only read about for a thousand years—the Second Avenue subway finally under construction, fencing extending halfway into the avenue like a narrow prison yard. I walked down to my first apartment at 309 E. 81st, the stoop now tricked out with brass railings and a door crested by a frosted fanlight, this walkup I rented for $175 a month in 1978, when I first arrived. I was twenty-three, newly married, and a new father.

I saw the bar sign in a window—Brady's Bar & Grill—at the corner of 82nd and 2nd Ave., just as I saw it warmly beckoning me four decades ago, a guy on his own, with, typically, about five dollars in his pocket, looking for company, for warmth and a drink. I ended up finding something of a home, an Irish bar, owned by Danny Brady, tended by fellows I got to know, from all over Ireland via Sunnyside, Queens. My five dollars could get me three or four drafts with a buyback and still leave something for a tip. And so there it was again, spiffed up now, and opening at noon, an NFL Sunday. I walked in. Transformed—a pool table, a few booths rather than a scatter of cheap tables and rickety chairs, and a young American bartender who looked like he was a gym rat rather than a faded fighter in a dress shirt huffing down Salems or the wiry alcoholic from Kilkenny, with his brogue and his narrow tie, as I was accustomed to seeing work the stick back in the day.

As I sat in the empty tavern, the sunlight raking in through the plate-glass window bringing out of the shadows the mesmerizing grain of a polished wooden bar top, I thought of where I was, where I had been, and how I got here, or there. Seeing me lost in my own reverie, the opening-up bartender didn't bother and instead started his setups and cutting his fruit. He turned on the televisions—there used to be one, now there were six. I took my leave after a coffee "on the house" and walked around the neighborhood where I first had a little son. We rolled him, his mother and I did, in a stroller up and down these streets in a season just like this, the leaves gold and the air sweet and the avenues filled with visual delights and on to Central Park past the

Metropolitan Museum and to the pathways into the park
lined with big trees and sweetened by music and the smells
of things growing and alive filling the air. My son, now in
his mid-forties, would cry to be reminded of being in New
York City, of being a child, of those golden leaves, of a city
park full of music and languages and his parents, all of it, all
of us, surrounded by large buildings, like sentinels of kind
protection that are no longer the sentinels that watch his
every move.

Bosch of *The Wayfarer* and *The Haywains* back-
To-back triptychs as one folding screen
From the 16th century, Bosch
Himself from 's-Hertogenbosch, in Brabant,
Netherlands, the town colloquially known as Den Bosch,
    contraction of the Dutch
"des Hertogen bosch," meaning "The Duke's forest"—Bois
    le-Duc in French,
bring on the boys, girls,
the stacks, stacks of wood,
paper of the wood, the pulp bound
In stacks, piled high on wagons (or wains), in racks, in
books, of wood. All wander in the forests,
shuffling leaves, that sound, a windfall away.

○ ○ ○ ○ ○

I once wrote a kind of memoir. I titled it "Finishing Ulysses,"
and it began like this:

I've spent much of my life trying to make sense of a mistake.

I've spent the rest of my life trying to escape the consequences. Or control them.

"Trying to make sense" does not mean simply a matter of thinking it through, though it is partially that.

Some of it is a matter of acting.

Taking action to redeem the mistake, to erase it, to have it be forgiven, forgotten. Escaped, if you will. Or managed.

Punishing.

I've done a lot of that.

I have to sort it out.

The mistake?

Marrying too young and for the wrong reason—fear.

Fear of what?

Fear of never finding a degree of intimacy in which my shortcomings would be accepted.

So that I could get on to the work of life, whatever it would be.

Fear that without intimacy, my hunger for it would get me killed.

And ruin the work, whatever it would be.

So I acted.

My mistake.

In the end I gave up a child.

As I had been given up.

I struggled with my ambitions and challenges in the New York workforce, in poorly paid entry-level positions which I nonetheless highly valued. I was no doubt the only editor at Brady's Bar & Grill, but so what? I never went downtown or to midtown where I might find poets or trade house editors; I didn't even know about it. I was happy to know where I was, and to get to know it, and I walked most everywhere, it saved money and was my first real tour of a fascinating city—in which I was born. I knew that I was not far from where my parents picked me up for the very first time.

I still have the letter. I recall correcting the date in my own hand. My correspondent, "Sr. Lillian Phelan, MSW," from the New York Foundling Hospital, had forgotten that we were in a new year, 1979, when dating her letter to me, "January 1978."

I had asked the Foundling by letter to please supply me with any information they could about my birth parents. The Foundling, where I'd been picked up at five weeks by John and Eleanor Coffey in 1954, was on East 68th Street, only fifteen blocks away. I felt I was getting closer to home.

Sister Lillian gave me background information, not identifying, but every little bit couldn't help but identify me a little more. The information spilled across five typewritten paragraphs, with words oddly capitalized as if plucked from a filled-out form, prompts and headings vanished.

My mother's name was Virginia—no last name, of course. "She was of Irish American Heritage and a College Graduate."

She had a Fair complexion, Brown eyes and Dark Brown hair.

She was on the small side, 5 ft. 3 in. tall, 123 lbs.

I was given her birth date—I noted she turned fourteen the day the Japanese bombed Pearl Harbor.

"She majored in English and Drama. She took Voice Lessons."

She was from the "North East Section of the U.S."

From a very large family, fourth from the youngest of nine children.

The "alleged" father was a freelance writer with "two years of College," he too "of Irish American Heritage" and from "the North East section of the U.S."

Five feet seven, about 150 pounds, "Fair complexion, Blue eyes and Brown hair."

Delivery was "difficult, by Low Forceps," perhaps explaining the scar on my forehead.

I noticed that I weighed the same at birth as my first son did.

"Your parents were not interested in marriage and felt that adoption would be the best plan for you."

Virginia married a friend "whom she'd stayed in touch with from college."

Several months after the adoption took place, the New York Foundling had me returned for some testing.

I was declared "fully average" with "an incipient social smile."

As I endured—and abetted—the marital tumult that was unraveling my own most immediate and young family (arguments, tantrums, money woes, lack of parenting skills), I attended to the search for my original family. Whom was I from? Did I have sisters and brothers out there, a famous father, a criminal father, a brilliant mother, an alcoholic mother? Who was Virginia and who was the—*my*—alleged father? I was from where in the "North East United States" Boston, New York, Hartford, Amherst? Lowell? Did it matter? I thought it did. To someone, perhaps to me. Answers to these questions might be answers to who I was or would

become. Or could become, in search of a sistering, a
brothering, a filiation, a parent.

∘ ∘ ∘ ∘ ∘

"The brig Covenant [from RLS's Kidnapped]. *I go in quest
of my inheritance. Portmanteau for a voyage—hazel wand—
firings—tattered military coat and so on. Are the children asleep?
All who read must cross the divide—one from the other. Towards
whom am I floating? I'll tie a rope round your waist if you say
who you are. Remember we are traveling as relations.
"Well it's the way of the world."*
—Susan Howe, *The Midnight*, p. 146

I might be in the birth records for the City of New York, I
reckoned. And now I lived there. On a visit home, which was
Saranac, NY, 335 miles north, I asked my mother for my birth
certificate. I told her I needed to renew my passport, which
indeed would expire in 1980, not that I was going anywhere.
This of course was an amended certificate—my name as
Coffey, my parents as John and Eleanor Coffey.

"I" might be in the birth records . . .

There were no Michael John Coffeys in the birth records of
New York City for 1954—not with Michael John Coffey's birth
date. Michael John Coffey asked a question of a librarian in
the Genealogy room, a woman with a southern accent. She
told him that there would be a number on his *amended* birth
certificate, and that number, if he could find it in the birth
records, would tell him who I was—his name at birth.

26

He took down the two volumes from 1954; the names of the babies born that year in the five boroughs were alphabetical by last name—I could be anywhere. But one of the columns for each entry was, of course, date of birth. His and mine—11/11, four consecutive ones—was easy to spot in columns of numbers. And there, in volume 1, page 67, column three, was who I (once) was:

Bradley, Mark   11 11 54   M   45277

Him.

Name, birth date, gender—and the five-digit number. I had found my name in the only place in the world it was written. "45277" is what let Coffey lay claim to that identity, for that was indeed the number on Coffey's amended birth certificate. And likely, the last name of "Virginia" was "Bradley."

I did not like the name *Mark*. "Mark" would mark me as bland, patrician—it wasn't far from "milk"—and having known only one Mark in my childhood, a quiet Methodist boy named Mark White, my name as "Mark" drained all the color for sure. Bradley? No better. That was a first name, like Thomas or Scott. It seemed to have no history to it, or character, and seemed thin on ethnicity. It didn't at all seem Irish. "Mark Bradley" to me was vanilla. It was a fake name, like the names callers from collection agencies give you on the phone, or used to—the James Stones and John Barkers. That's how I saw it. No. I was someone, but I was no Mark Bradley, and I was no evangelist. I was *un*Marked. Unremarked, but in one volume of city records, by the one mark of me in an archive I was marked. The archive whispered my name.

⁓ ⁓ ⁓ ⁓ ⁓

Only two nights after the Beckett and Bagels event, I went to hear the poet read—but really I went to look at her right hand.

I said hello, and I saw her hands, and her right hand, and the ring finger of said hand, and I shook it, hello. Her Celtic hand.

I could not stay for the reading, for the man who read before her was *unbearable*.

And because I was only there to see her hands, her right hand, the ring finger, or the pinkie, which I saw, and unwilling to endure a long preface to one man's engagement with a single article on schizophrenia from 1919, in that overheated bookstore, in wait for his promised long poem about it, I left, to the cool of Prince Street. I'd seen her right hand, I'd held it. The ring finger was not bent sharply like Beckett's, broken by the fascia's contraction; and a digit did not dart like a pencil in my hand, when I shook it, but rather, the pinkie dropped down, at nearly 90 degrees, straight at the floor, even as I watched her later, standing on the street (I'd fortified myself at nearby Fanelli's), holding her papers, her right hand pressed against her waist, elbow crooked, that right hand with long, thin pinkie finger pointed right down, at the sidewalk, as if broken.

⁓ ⁓ ⁓ ⁓ ⁓

Because Beckett wrote, "One day she had the impudence to announce she was with child."

And because, "I summoned up my remaining strength and said, 'Abort, abort . . . ' "

Because he wrote, "She had drawn back the curtain for a clear view of all her rotundities. I saw the mountain, impassable, cavernous, secret, where from morning to night I'd hear nothing but the wind, the curlews, the clink like distant silver of the stone-cutters' hammers. I'd come out in the daytime to the heather and gorse, all warmth and scent, and watch at night the distant city lights, if I chose, and the other lights, the lighthouses and lightships my father had named for me, when I was small, and whose names I could find again, in my memory, if I chose, that I knew. From that day forth things went from bad to worse, to worse and worse."

"If it's lepping, it's not mine," he wrote. All these things in the story, sometimes called a "nouvelle," "First Love."

Because years later—in the 1970s—Mary Manning Howe returned to Dublin to tell all who would listen that her first child was his. The nouvelle was about her, said Mary, or Molly as she was known. "I was the first love," she said. This told to me by a Dublin professor who was there at the time.

And no one chose to believe her.

> *"Because she was brushed aside at the scene of inheritances."*
> —Susan Howe quoting Helene Cixous on Gertrude Stein

Because the mail today brought a book about the Irish poet Brian Coffey and I can hardly stop reading it as a snowstorm falls around us in the country, where it is white right now but for the black of the skeletal trees and iron fencing, the only noise in the otherwise solid silence the occasional snowplow laboring up the hill scything its harvest of white powder to the shoulder. Brian Coffey, whom I did not meet and whose couple of letters to me I no longer have, was so gracious, alive then in Southampton with his wife, Bridget, and—I did not know at the time—nine children was willing to meet me and Oralia, my wife, coming down from Leeds so that I could ask him questions about *Advent*, his long poem on which I was writing my master's thesis. But Oralia's morning sickness kept us from taking the train down to see him, and we had to cancel. Two months later, when my first son was born, I wrote to Brian Coffey to tell him that we had given Joshua the middle name Brian.

Because Brian Coffey wrote to me that they are two strong warrior names, Joshua and Brian, from the Bible and from Ireland.

Because Beckett to MacGreevy, March 7, 1937: "I had a letter from Brian who mentioned he had heard from you. He remains very mysteriously under some wooden sword of Damocles, says he told his father he was dead & so on. How fortunate to have a father to say that one is dead to. . . . Mary Manning writes from Boston that her belly is enormous. Doors open in May."

Because, how casually: "in May"? Doing the math . . .

Because, "Doors open in May"?

Because, Is this how two Irishmen refer to giving birth?

The poet/baby was due in May. The mother said so, to Sam.

Because my son turned out indeed to be a warrior.

∘ ∘ ∘ ∘ ∘

The son texts me on yet another phone:

In the end, I'm an outsider
in this city. I'm formidable
sure. Smart. Fearless.
But some see me as a thing
to be removed so that they can move
forward. And they have no
honor. None.

If one's life and sobriety
are at risk, the smart thing
to do would be to get out.

What exactly do you mean, Father,
get out?

∘ ∘ ∘ ∘ ∘

Without words what are facts?
—Susan Howe

*In my writing I have often explored ideas of what constitutes
an official version of events as opposed to a former version
in imminent danger of being lost.*
—Howe

*When a piece is really alive and going well,
you give yourself over to coincidence.*
—Howe to Joan Jonas

Take Mark—the name of [Susan] *Howe's father and son, a
central figure in* The Secret History of the Dividing Line.
*The mark (mar, from secret history, 1) of an enclosure. The
border between. That which mars the undifferentiated,
soils the soil, establishes identity, fixes territory, announces
sovereignty* [sic]. *For what's been marked is claimed,
possessed—the sign of a stake (state). At the same time
a mark is a token, that which stands for something else,
the visible trace of a sign, metaphor for a word, substitute for
a signature and so standing for a name.*
—Charles Bernstein,
from *The Difficulties,*
The Susan Howe Issue (1989), p. 84

ооооо

At the end of my first (and last) Modern Language Association session, NYC, January 2018, a session on Beckett and "The Discourse of Psychoanalysis," I asked a question in the Q and A of one of three speakers—Daniela Caselli, a prominent Beckettian, whose paper dealt with the "abortive texts" in Beckett. There was a lot of talk of his abhorrence of gestation and birth, his hatred of children, of menses and the like. My question, then: would it make a difference if Beckett had actually fathered a child, or suspected he had? The next morning, a colleague in attendance asked me in an email why it mattered to me.

Dear L—

Being an adoptee, a literary person and a writer, I know that I am especially sensitive to the issue of literary inheritance. I spent many decades pursuing my identity through writing, through the lives of writers, through literature, looking for clues as to who I was in the evidence of my own practice and the manners of my reading. Whether I have discovered a sense of my self through this process or imagined it I cannot say. But I can say it is one, the other, or a mixture of both.

When the rumor of Beckett having fathered the poet Susan Howe reached me some ten years ago, I had already read much of the work of each writer. I began then to consider their work under the lamplight of my own interest in literary and biological inheritance, for indeed I had spent a lot of time imagining a parent of mine whose literary or artistic predilections might be my own, as well as imagining how the literary or artistic practice of a surrendering parent might be affected by such an act. I was traveling in what adoption therapist Betty Jean Lifton called "the ghost kingdom," a magical world where possible siblings and parents move among the populace, lurk behind pillars, perhaps looking for you, or the opposite, you for them.

I can report that Howe's writing—to my eye—is full of references, however veiled and oblique, to a mystery of inheritances, to the "occult ferocity of origin," as she writes in the brilliant *Singularities*, though this element of her work, most prevalent in the more autobiographical of her texts like *The Midnight* but evident throughout, is not part of the critical discourse about her. I can also report that—to my eye—the writing of Beckett is full of references, however coarsely stated, to the tyranny of inheritance or influences ("cursed progenitor!"), though this element of his work, evident throughout, is very much part of the critical discourse about him. To a point. [Daniela] Caselli drew the line at that point, as have others. Hence your question: "What would it mean to know the answer to [my] question?"

Let me first clarify what I think the question should be. The question is not whether Beckett is Susan Howe's father. She has claimed that there is evidence—established in the 1990s—that he is not.

There is no reason for me to disbelieve her. The question is, then, twofold: how did it affect Susan Howe's evolving identity and practice as a writer to be in her fifties before discovering for sure who her father was—was he the American legal scholar, editor of the Oliver Wendell Holmes letters that she grew up with in Buffalo and Boston or the Irish Nobel laureate, her mother's friend from childhood, who lived In Paris? And secondly, if Susan was unsure for all that time, what was Beckett sure of, and how did the uncertainty, if he was not shielded from it, affect his work?

Did Beckett suspect that her uncertainty was a torment for her and her children? Did he suspect it affected her work? Did he know nothing but sense everything, at whatever level? Beckett died before the evidence (a DNA test) was generated.

Daniela is not the first to write about Beckett's discussion of abortion, abortive texts, and so on. But I find it baffling that on the same [MLA] panel that can talk about Beckett's sessions with [psychotherapist] Bion, which of course is inevitably in the context of his issues with the "savage love" of his mother, May, the possibility of his own fathering of a child is off limits. If someone could tell me that he did not suspect that Susan might be his child, I would leave it alone. But no one has or will. It is passed over in silence. Marty F and Jim K rely on funny math to dismiss the possibility that Beckett could be the father, but that is not the issue. The math does not appear to have been convincing enough to settle the case back in 1937, when Susan was born forty-one weeks after Mary left Ireland. (Beckett, incidentally, spent six of those nine months on his own wandering around Nazi Germany, on his mother's dime. A kind of halfhearted exile from the maternal?)

I believe that Susan Howe has insisted this issue is not for public discussion, and her wishes have largely been respected—I don't mention her by name in my earlier book on Beckett, though I do reference the issue. As for the Beckett estate, the possibility of an heir would be quite problematic, would it not?— hypothetically speaking? If Edward Beckett had expressed discomfort with the issue, given his power over copyright and performance rights to Beckett works, that would be respected as well.

If indeed there are letters that reveal Beckett's concern about having fathered a child, I can't agree that it would be irrelevant to the work—is it less important than Beckett attending a Jung lecture at Tavistock or reading *Nightwood* or having a preference for Eluard over Breton or Jack Yeats over André Masson? (I would agree that if he were indifferent to the matter, it would be of little interest to the work.) Should a biography be written of Howe one day, her concern about who her father was and her mother's inability or unwillingness to clear it up will be part of it, unless somehow enjoined. Whether there is any evidence that Beckett had even a clue I do not know—but I can tell you that no one has said there is or is not. As Daniela said in answer to my questions, "I don't go there." On this issue, perhaps Samuel Beckett is closed.

What meaning would it have for me (or us) if Beckett was aware of Susan Howe's uncertainty (of paternity)? (Think of *Godot*, which begins "Nothing to be done" and continues, "Nothing is certain when you're around," exchanges between our pseudocouple Didi and Gogo.) It might change how we view the unattended children that wander in and out of his works, often as messengers. We might consider this uncertainty as another element to his trauma that was channeled into the frenzy of writing just after the war that produced his central masterworks. It might reset or refresh the discussions about Beckett's relation to the body and the sexual act. Consider if he was aware of a young woman's torment across the Atlantic. We do know he was very sympathetic when faced with the struggles or sufferings of dear friends. Somehow, I think Arka's word "parallax" would apply—we might see the object (the texts, the subject) differently with this slight change in perspective.

I hope this clarifies my interest somewhat. In any event, thanks for *your* interest!

All the best,

Michael

·····

My son in the woods with a handgun.

Walked without being in light there was. Along tracks.
Tracks along the river, down from mountains, hills, down to
the sea. Walked without being to the sea.

Beach rose.

In light there was, still, returning still, as always. Light goes,
comes, without being, walked without being, along, within,
all the same, breathing.

All the same, and then some, all around, a supply, the
knowledge of air, taken on faith, a creation, a gift. No, a
condition, everywhere, mountain to sea, without being.

The last person but one, or but one but one, the question that
occupies the mind, the all-mind, the land then. The question
of the land. Toward which

these boots, soft camel hair without, within, another beast,
fur of. These losses weathered.

Boots seen as self, always in view if not *on* then *near*, as self is
near, felt within and without, without being.

And sash, no order to this, now at sash. Loyal embracer,
made of kinds of hemp or what rope might ever have to be to
do, a monk's cord. Chastity.

Dragged across the plain, the sand, whether boot or sash or staff, one long scribble, the wandering line bare of information, long on meaning.

No time like the precedent, ha ha, for now. But space it out.

One coin what realm to be read with the fingers. Pressed from silver by other hands unknown with punch and hammer now read with thumb and forefinger, a history. Tree and bird, the branches, the wings, those letters, what are they, Greek, *chi*, something, *ro*, perhaps, Son of God, ha! That's a wreath. And there *alla y omega*, be all end all, all things, this already known. This in a museum in Bilbão. Jose Francisco told us to come. But this is anywhere.

Begun where was. An axiom. All do, but where is where? Or is it *when* is where? One when, the only when in play, at a time, was a where, in the mountains, near a stream. Water again, never dash it, always babbling, like a language, or roaring like another, or long slow crashes, the sea full of syllables, remember, that poem,

those sounds, sound itself, emerging from a reading of Paul Metcalf, Melville's grandson, sound always, even silence ever rare is heard. Most common the sounds of whatever thing trailing words of a language, the name, were there a name, over and over in variations, no matter, only. Sound, never ever none till. No name is still a name.

Is there body? Not here. No matter. But what of boots and sash, of shod, clad? What of fingering silver? Whence the miracle of coinage? Yes to body, but not here.

Baggage, body. But there a girl unable to part from her beau, the beau in Bilbão, it is their mouths that touch, their eyes that inspect each other's eyes, each with hands in the other's hands, alive to each other head to foot, nearly twanging on the portico, this memory sluicing through.

Purpose the body, it's the only way. Embody the fiction, little choice elsewise but mathematics or music, words, if not bound to the body are more resonant there, to be heard, not a bad thing, incarnate. Fill an empty void sodden with sounds, with more sounds, sounds of emptiness. Vast stretch of time, Beckett knew, how it is, to end, or knew how it is to the end more proper.

There is that sound just now, meaning then, just then, very near and receding then, a click. The sound of a light switch, turning on, or off, all the same sound but one brings light and the other dark, all the same, the same click, the future plunging into the past. Whether candlepower plus sounds and some decor or a page of text swimming into the clear or a mother's hand and her voice coming with the new fallen dark to minister, the room alive now to other sounds, other tickings, of a clock, the weather dripping or the house settling, it is all the same now, here on the empty road winding by into the future but right now present—no, plunging.

This time how long this time? Live for a moment or a second? Choose. Live for a day, one day, live for a day, this your day, at the end it will darken, already it is, see?

No surprises, just darkening. Relax. The day enjoyed, and the night, and the never over, the never after, always one at one time, all at one time, just a day. Sufficient unto the day is the evil thereof, my father would say. Good-bye Dad.

What is the other without the one? The one. One equals one, no other. No other one. One none or all. One one one one.

Columns of air. Silos of void.

∘ ∘ ∘ ∘ ∘

There is an unpublished bit of prose in the Beckett Archive at Reading that I cannot quote for copyright reasons. Part of what is called Beckett's "grey canon," the text is titled "The Way," dated 14 May 1987, written when Beckett was eighty-one. I will describe it. Thirty-seven sentences. Grammatical subjects hardly present, the gist of it all the tracing of a path to the top of a rise and down the other side, in a figure 8, on foot, a mile an hour, mist, half-light, the will, however briefly, set free. There is some regret expressed that the seconds have not been counted. (Oh, the math!) There is no sign of remains and no sign of no remains. Another Beckett piece that pitches time and marks it but without narrative, like the short play *Footfalls*, with the repetitive pacing back and forth, or like the short play *Rockaby*, with the repetitive rocking back and forth. Somehow the sun at rest. An infinity sign in Beckett's hand breaks the text midway. Life as a figure 8, then executed in ascent. And in descent.

Beckett would be dead in thirty months.

My son in the woods with a handgun. On the run. Trying to leave no trace. Walking on loose sand or bedrock. No tracks.

○ ○ ○ ○ ○

In America a person named Chris Marker could be from any place.

I'm being eaten alive, the son texts.

> *It is fun to be hidden but horrible not to be found.*
> —Howe, from *The Midnight*, p. 127

> *Somewhere else I read [that] his surname may simply be a reference to magic markers, because they highlight or mark a text at the same time you can see through it.*
> —Howe, *Sorting Facts; Or, Nineteen Ways of Looking at Marker*, p. 56

Is a hi-lighter magic?
Or is it what language (according to L=A=N=G=U=A=G=E) is not supposed to be: transparent?

Susan Howe's imagination seems almost entirely rooted in the colonial history of New England and its expression and reflection in literature as she finds them in the region's preciously held archives. Her enchantment with her very Irish mother's roots and imagination is over time eclipsed by her boldly staked claim to Bay Colony history, religious practice, and the transcendent violence that accompanied the establishment of a Puritan God and the "City on a Hill." Howe trains a powerful glare on the vicious treatment of women and Native Americans bound up in the John Cotton/Cotton Mather/John Winthrop/Thomas Dudley vision of an American exceptionalism. She can't get enough of this: critically, admiringly, disruptively, single-mindedly, boldly, she thrashes about in those archives near to home looking for lost threads, pages, injustice, genius, and ultimately a gendered justice.

> *During World War II he may have served as a resistance fighter*
> *during the occupation of France . . .*
> —Howe on Chris Marker in *Sorting Facts;*
> *Or, Nineteen Ways of Looking at Marker*

Who? *Chris Marker*

After the war he contributed poetry, political commentary, music criticism, short stories, and film essays . . .

Who? *Not Beckett. Chris Marker.*

But why not?

Chris Marker, a most American-sounding name for one Christian François Bouche-Villeneuve, that name sounding so fake you begin to question the veracity of both names. *Mark*er dabbles in the visible and -*bouche* rounds into sounds like a new town empty of meaning.

There is an obsession with facts in Howe's thinking about Marker, and an obsession with facts in all her work despite a distrust of them, not so much that facts as facts are not true but that they obscure other truths, some not factual but also not false. Perhaps "obscure" doesn't always serve, as the verb "to obscure" connotes intentionality, perhaps occludes would do in some cases, or occult or occultation, a word favored by Samuel Beckett in an unpublished work, where something occults a view of something else, as in a parallax.

Howe's book on Marker appears at first rather to be an anomaly in her oeuvre in being ostensibly about a 20th-century figure, or several of them, all of them filmmakers, documentarians and Marxists—Dziga Vertov, Tarkovsky, and the Frenchman Marker. However, and more typical of Howe's work generally, this sixty-four-page chapbook published by New Directions is also about loss, written under the sign of yet another death, in this case that of her second husband, David von Schlegel, who succumbed at seventy-two from a stroke. In the grieving process that constitutes the zigzag through-line to *Sorting Facts*, Howe seems to find some solace in her signature tracing of inheritances, in this case one that runs back from her

apparent subject—documentarians—to the Russian poet
Mayakovsky and before that to Walt Whitman, Melville,
Dickinson, and before that, to Howe's own packed private
cabinet of American Puritan theologians (Mather, Edwards),
up through a bunch of other American-born protestants,
Emerson, Eliot, Crane (Hart), H.D., Moore, Williams,
Stevens, to Olson, to Cage and to Howe herself. These
are all in some sense, she says, practitioners of montage
interested in exploring the means of their own production.
These are interesting thoughts, and Howe, as in all of her
work, opens her texts to scrutiny as to historical sources and
contemporary personal and social context—and to emotion.
She revels in finding the ghosts in the textual fabric, in
libraries, in marginalia. As Olson spotted Shakespeare in
Moby-Dick, Howe detects the pallid image of Irish poet James
Clarence Mangan in the figure of Melville's Bartleby. I am
of the mind now, after years of skepticism about Howe's
projects, and even more years of reading her, that she is
certainly a legitimate inheritor of the lineage into which she
has placed herself.

> *Is it possible that I too am acting out a role? The role of seeker*
> *after film truth? Do I really seek truth? Perhaps this too is a*
> *mask, which I myself don't realize.*
> —Dziga Vertov, 1937

Is it possible that Howe (b. 1937) too is acting out a role, the
role of being a sorter of facts? Does she really seek the truth
or is the belief in facts itself a mask, and facts in fact do not
exist, cannot be found, or are obscured to us?

Bearer of lethal invisible material, Howe writes, in *Sorting Facts.*

Surely nonfiction filmmakers sometimes work intuitively by factual telepathy, she writes in *Sorting Facts.*

I call poetry factual telepathy, she writes in *Sorting Facts.*

If facts are to be telepathically communicated through poetry—or film—where are the facts telepathically coming from? Or going to? I write.

∘ ∘ ∘ ∘ ∘

[This montage mine.]

∘ ∘ ∘ ∘ ∘

Facts:

Howe on her mother Mary Manning Howe: "She loved to embroider facts. Facts were cloth to her. Maybe lying is how she knew she was alive because she felt trapped by something ruthless in her environment and had to beat the odds."—Howe, *The Midnight*, p. 76

> *The jester walked in the garden:*
> *The garden had fallen still;*
> *He bade his soul rise upward*
> *And stand on her window-sill.*

"We loved to read that one together [Yeats's "The Cap and Bells" from *The Wind Among the Reeds* (1899)].

"So when I read it now all the words fall softly over what we believed then and desired. It was like a ballad though not for singing. 'The Cap and Bells' was our lantern to light a place of separation."

What is a "place of separation"? And why would a poor Yeats poem bring light to it?

It says "Michael Coffey," in the florid script I used at the time, another me trying to be another me. It said "19 Otley Road, Harrogate HG2 0DJ." It said "Oct 1976." My first marriage.

The
COLLECTED POEMS
of
W. B. YEATS

LONDON
MACMILLAN & CO LTD
1961

> *The jester walked in the garden:*
> *The garden had fallen still;*
> *He bade his soul rise upward*
> *And stand on her window-sill.*

It rose in a straight blue garment,
When owls began to call:
It had grown wise-tongued by thinking
Of a quiet and light footfall;

But the young queen would not listen;
She rose in her pale night-gown;
She drew in the heavy casement
And pushed the latches down.

He bade his heart go to her,
When the owls called out no more;
In a red and quivering garment
It sang to her through the door.

It had grown sweet-tongued by dreaming
Of a flutter of flower-like hair;
But she took up her fan from the table
And waved it off on the air.

'I have cap and bells,' he pondered,
'I will send them to her and die';
And when the morning whitened
He left them where she went by.

She laid them upon her bosom,
Under a cloud of her hair,
And her red lips sang them a love-song
Till stars grew out of the air.

She opened her door and her window,
And the heart and the soul came through,
To her right hand came the red one,
To her left hand came the blue.

They set up a noise like crickets,
A chattering wise and sweet,
And her hair was a folded flower
And the quiet of love in her feet.

Howe wrote, in *The Midnight*, that the Yeats poem "is a dream poem in which a jester tries to impress a young queen by sending her his heart and soul, which she waves away; he then sends her his jester's cap and bells, which she accepts, and presses to her bosom, and sings a song, until his heart and soul return . . ."

"They set up a noise like crickets," wrote Yeats, of the chattering of disembodied heart and soul.

A noise like crickets.
No, like leaves.
Where are the children?

○ ○ ○ ○ ○

Turns out I sent my son *Jesus' Son* three times, over the years, twice forgetting that I had already done so, always freshly convinced that Denis Johnson's depiction of American life *in extremis* and the rough beauty of his language was just the thing that would give my wayward boy courage, just the thing to help him realize, perhaps, that his life, at last, could be transformed into a kind of art, no matter his hardships, his hard living—in fact *with* benefit of hardships and hard living. I believe I did a similar thing with *The Inferno*, twice at least sending him the Robert Pinsky translation, to one prison or another, convinced that here in Dante was a system imaginable in a language that could contain us all. The young kid who liked violent video games and boxing was entranced by Dante's spectacular subterranean chambers outfitted for meting out forms of torture as a divine justice worthy of God or the Mario Brothers or Mike Tyson.

"You can't burgulate a forgotten, empty house," Wayne tells the skeptical narrator pal, aka Fuckhead, in Johnson's story "Work," in *Jesus' Son*.

Turns out the empty house is one of a dozen abandoned structures along a riverbank development, and it used to be Wayne's. The two men are there to *work*; Wayne has brought his tools, Fuckhead drove them in his "sixty-dollar banger," their goal the copper wiring and other salvageable scraps from the house. They toil somehow through heroin highs, vomiting every once in a while ("a thimbleful of gray bile"). They hear and then see a motorboat coming upriver. It is towing aloft a kite with a naked red-haired woman harnessed in ("a beautiful thing," declares Wayne). Later, Wayne and Fuckhead drive to see a woman in a farmhouse a good distance away. She comes out to the porch. One and the same redhead. Turns out this is Wayne's wife. Wayne and she talk. Then the two men leave.

"As nearly as I could tell," reflects Fuckhead, "I'd wandered into some sort of dream that Wayne was having about his wife, and his house."

Turns out my son is a three-time felon and addict, with several more minor infractions. A long rap sheet. He has done time in three Indiana state prisons and four Indiana county jails. His mother and I split up when he was two and a half—I stayed in Manhattan, she returned with Josh to her parents in Indiana; she went on to have two other boys before dying of hypothermia and alcohol toxicity when this son of mine was eleven. He visited me, I visited him, over the years, but I did not raise him. Eventually, I visited him wherever incarcerated—Westville, Michigan City, Westville again, Elkhart County, St. Joe County, Kosciusko. Some place farther south I missed.

He got in trouble just after high school graduation, in 1996. He was nineteen. I bought him an expensive suit from Barney's for the trial, in hope that a sharp appearance would make a difference with the judge. He got a two-and-a-half- to eight-year sentence for assault and did half the minimum, fifteen months. He then tried his luck in New York City, living with me in my new family, but got arrested twice for fighting (both times in Union Square Station). Having fled back to Indiana, he worked over the hood of a taxi with a baseball bat in a dispute over a fare home from a company Christmas party he'd been asked to leave, got involved in a violent bar fight a few years later where a man was badly injured, had altercations involving a pistol and a junkie girlfriend, and fell into meth addiction along the way.

He's been on the run, turned in, busted; he's cut his wrists, searched for buried treasure, lived in the woods, searched for fossils, never shaking what turned into an addiction and never probing some deep losses, as he would agree. He told me he last saw a dentist when he was ten.

He's out now, for now, as I write. "Pulled these out of an abandoned house . . . sold them today for 145.00"—a pair of tabletop pinball machines with *Star Trek* themes are pictured in his text message. "Not a crime," he adds, "to salvage these the property is in ruins. And not on Private Property the place has no doors."

What did he say to me about Dante? I remember he thought the Pinsky superior to the Ciardi. I sent him the book in 1997. Amazon was the best thing that happened to readers in prison—they let those packages right in (paperbacks only). Years later, after two prison stints, now with his partner and getting by raising their two girls, a good period it seemed— he had a mortgage, a car loan, and a demanding machinist job on a CNC milling machine at which he excelled—I sent him Beckett's *Endgame*, as he'd had a flare for drama in high school. He performed monologues in some kind of scholastic competition, tournaments on the road, reading out Mamet and Tennessee Williams and Clifford Odets. Near my office, there was a bookstore that had a Tony Kushner event, and Mr. Kushner inscribed a copy to my son, warmly. It was an early edition of *Angels in America*, I think, now lost to the chaos of my son's life, like every other thing I gave him. But *Endgame*, years later, with such experience under this belt I thought my son would relate to—the humor, the pathos, the desperate straits. (Hamm: What do you see? Clov: I see my light dying.) He said, "Dad, this is all from Dante, isn't it?" Spot on. Did he pause, I wonder, at "Cursed progenitor"?

I put him in a story once. He was at large then, on the run, through the woods, toward me, no, toward "Liam," Liam in his mountain cabin, as far as he could be from anything and still call it his—or home. In my story, titled "Sons," a son is forever. They leave you, if they leave you, though did I leave my father—which father?—the one I knew, the one who raised me? Yes I left, I left home, and yes I loved the father I left behind, the father who raised me and showed me his things and his thinking, in a million moments, I was lucky to have them, and him. The other father I never knew, he was kept from me, he is no one to me. But I heard he loved Joyce and jazz, and what do you know, now I do too. My story's last word was "Him."

My son in a field with a handgun.

I put him in a story once.

○ ○ ○ ○ ○

In Samuel Beckett's novel *Watt*, one of the characters (Arsene) undergoes a sudden change in his outlook. Beckett writes:

"But in what did the change consist? . . . What was changed, if my information is correct, was the sentiment that a change, other than a degree, had taken place. What was changed was existence off the ladder. Do not come down the ladder, Ifor, I haf taken it away."

Beckett was asked if this is a direct allusion to Wittgenstein's statement about his own propositions building to a place where one "throws away the ladder, after you have climbed up on it." The mock German accent was considered a further clue. But Beckett said no. He hadn't read Wittgenstein at the time, and that the ladder is a reference to "a Welsh joke" (that he did not specify), making the pronunciation not German but Welsh.

I passed the question on to a Welshman I know who in turn passed it on to Welsh-speaking friends but "not a smile was raised." This is what was said—*Apropos the Welsh joke, no one I have contacted knows anything about Ifor bach. I think you can assume he was making it up using a Welshified accent and a name like Ifor. Although he should've used a double f in 'haf.' Perhaps he was taking the piss out of the Welsh or having a little chuckle at his own joke.*

In Howe's book of poetry *The Liberties* (1983), a book she called "my goodbye to Dublin . . . [a] book that an Irish person would find . . . laughable," she ends the second of three sections with that very construction, with some variation:

I can re

trace

my steps

I who

crawl

between thwarts

Do not come down the ladder

ifor I

haveaten

it a

way

What could this mean?

But for the -*eat*- in *haveaten*, you have *haven*. New Haven? Or: what ladder is being removed, that's the question. As I am beginning to appreciate, both artists are in a league of their own in basing their works on subtraction of content, or obstruction, or sharp opposition, and dismantlings, with Howe defacing text into illegibility, with Beckett stressing inaudibility at times, or nonsense. Both trafficking in the indecipherable.

From the interview with Janet Ruth Fallon in *The Difficulties* issue on Susan Howe:

Howe: "If you can't decide where your allegiance lies you feel permanently out. I had to feel at home somewhere and I think that was another reason I found it was so urgent for me to write the [Emily] Dickinson book. In fact, I haven't been to Dublin now in five years. Maybe *The Liberties* was my goodbye to Dublin. I'm always sure about that book, that an Irish person would find it laughable. My children have the same love for Ireland as I do."

Me: Has the ladder back to Ireland been eaten (erased), creating for her a new *haven*? Her New Haven—home now to her beloved Sterling Library and the Beinecke—acquired from the Quinnipiac in 1638 by a Puritan minister with five hundred congregants in return for bowls, hatchets, shears, and blankets.

○ ○ ○ ○ ○

Howe's 1983 *The Liberties* centers on the question of parentage. Was Hester Johnson fathered by Sir William Temple or by Edward Johnson, one of the stewards on Temple's estate in Surrey? "[I]t was rumored from very early on that the bright and pretty child . . . strikingly resembled Temple, [and] was his natural daughter." Born in 1680 in England, Hester grew close to her tutor, the young Jonathan Swift, who taught her to read, among other things. She and Swift remained extremely close until Hester, known as Stella to Swift (who liked to give his woman friends "allegorical names"), predeceased him in 1727. Swift would live another seventeen years; they are buried next to each other beneath the flagstones in St. Patrick's

Cathedral in The Liberties section of Dublin, where Swift had become Dean.

Howe's text is dedicated to her namesake and maternal grandmother, Susan Manning, who, incidentally, was friendly with Samuel Beckett's parents, Bill and May Beckett. *The Liberties*, the title a shorthand reference to a section of southwest Dublin that once housed predominantly Protestant and Huguenot stock but which in time gave over to a more Catholic and working-class (and rebel) neighborhood, begins with the prose narrative of Swift's role in the Temple household—as secretary to William Temple and tutor to Hester. Howe includes details of Hester's inheritance from Temple (400 pounds) and her long tenure as an employee of Swift. Swift, of course, ascends through the Church of Ireland to a variety of important posts and becomes the famous author of satire, including the ironic "Modest Proposal for Preventing the Children of Poor People from Being a Burthen to Their Parents or Country." Hester, unsure of who her father is, becomes devoted to Dean Swift, fourteen years her elder, a devotion that seemed to be requited, as the sixty-five letters between them suggest.

Howe begins with a straightforward introduction of the Stella-Swift relationship. Although miscounting the number of letters, Howe economically summarizes the odd relationship between the great writer/clergyman and the woman of dubious parentage, who was attractive and more importantly skilled at managing household affairs. Howe also includes a section titled "Stella's Portrait," descriptive text, telegraphic as if in a hurry, probably to convey that here is a woman marginalized (and renamed) in a history told by men about men. Her social skills, love of horses, her punning, her hair color ("raven black") and feistiness (she once shot a prowler) are listed in one paragraph, followed by the terse stand-alone line: "No authentic portrait exists."

This is a theme that Howe pursues in subsequent works, most famously in *My Emily Dickinson*, her reclamation of Dickinson as a singular literary genius ill-served by male editors, but also in her study of captivity narratives, featuring experiences by white European women taken by Native American tribes in New England. This theme of disinheritances suffered by women in the normal course of things with famous men prevails throughout Howe's corpus and is part of her own story, as she tells it, as the true nature of her parentage appears to have been a fugitive, elusive fact.

The "portrait" section in *The Liberties* continues in pedestrian prose to limn the circle of Swift and Stella—their movements, their halting and covert courtship, their possible secret marriage, up to her death as "a spinster." Howe includes her speculation that the reason Swift and Stella might not have wed, if they in fact did not, is that Swift, with his own doubts about paternity, combined with the closeness of the Swift and Temple families, considered it a possibility that he and Stella were related—and that they—the two of them—knew it. This kind of suspicion bordering on fantasy is rife in the worlds of orphans, adoptees, and illegitimate children, for whom kingdoms of imaginary relations abound, improbably projected far and near. Howe finishes this section with Swift's epitaph, upon his tombstone, set in the flagstones right next to that of Stella, in the southwest corner of St. Patrick's in Dublin.

○ ○ ○ ○ ○

He is outside now, as in he's "on the outside," *for now*, ironically *making walls*; he knows how they are built and is still learning about the art of enclosure, but now for gardens in the few tony parts of South Bend. He has no papers, does not exist now, *for now*, as if (and why not?) this *now* can end. This is the only life in this story, crawling, throbbing in a rock garden of conjecture, I know it and am sorry for it, but I too must write my story. Even if he has a gun.

Now he's making me a drawing—of Samuel Beckett. Now he is telling me about Petoskey stones, found only in Michigan and northern Indiana. The stones are a fossil, of coral and a stone, somehow, with hexagonal patterns, tortoise-shell like. They are 350 million years old.

Now he is running a chain saw and a wood chipper. He doesn't believe in the Bible and detests those who do, except his grandmother. Whom he never sees because he has a serious problem with her caretaker.

My son is living either in a field near the local airport, or in a hotel for transients and addicts, which is conveniently near a Pizza Hut, I am told.

I fly out there from New York. Into the obnoxious South Bend airport, which sits asquat an empty field, as do many airports, and most prisons, architectures of waiting. Inside the "terminal" is a long desk empty of agents and graced by a big yellow Humvee nearby (locally made) that you can win in a raffle, plus a shop with Fightin' Irish merchandise (from diapers to a rocking chair) and a grim food counter with a prominent beer tap. I've been here before, many visits to my son's life.

I have reserved a medium-sized car with Avis but all they have left is a big SUV. After about five miles it has a flat tire. Turns out there is no spare. I have to abandon it and wait for a replacement. Appallingly, this takes two days. I spend the weekend in a hotel, eating at the closest restaurant, a Hooter's, where men drink heavily at a horseshoe bar, couples eat fried food and steaks at booths and tables, and the sorriest-looking women march around in ill-fitting halter tops, carrying three or four plates running up one arm and a brimming pitcher of beer in the other and you wish they'd show a lot less flesh, they look so cold and exposed. But they are unfailingly nice and working their butts off. I know I am in Trump country when some guy at the bar in a MAGA hat looks at me long enough to earn an acknowledging nod; something about my cashmere painter's coat, perhaps, registers as a threat to Carhartt and liberty. But the nod was enough, apparently. All eyes return to Alabama–LSU on the big screen. I turn down a shot of tequila with a grace that involves pointing to my watch. The next day I eat out of a vending machine and order some old-school Arthur Treacher's for delivery at dinnertime to the hotel.

I have heard that my son is living in a motel southwest of town. This from his aunt who will tell me things if asked. When I have four good wheels beneath me I go looking for his latest shelter. The Red Rock Inn is a two-story run of rooms with a plastic chair outside each door on the ground floor and a table and chairs on the narrow balconies of the second floor, $60 to $75 a night.

I have no clear idea if he is here, his phone is off, texts "did not send" and phone calls get a message saying "this number is not registered." I wait in the parking lot in my Ford Taurus that smells like men's cologne. English Leather? Is that still around? It's all over the steering wheel. I can feel the tickle of its alcohol suspension evaporating from my palms. I realize I should probably resume smoking cigarettes for this trip—as a disinfectant.

I am slung down low in my replacement vehicle—sunk "in my solitude," since there is a Duke Ellington special on the satellite radio's jazz channel—toward the back left of the Red Rock Inn parking lot, rain coming down in swaying curtains, though I have a good if grayed-out view of the motel and the rest of the lot as well as a view down Michigan Avenue, a country highway, one on which, maybe five miles farther east, I lived for a few months with my son's late mother, my first wife, before he was born. I could fall asleep in this girdle of rain.

I don't know what I am watching for other than for my son, whom I haven't seen in three or four years. Or what I am waiting for. Last time he was released I was there—he emerged with long black hair tied back in a ponytail, his face full of jagged features, his teeth, a scar, and still the nervous eyes and mouth, as if about to yell or flee or weep. That time, he had gotten himself *straight back in* the joint in the space of a few months, as if refusing to be born.

I am here, though unannounced, to see what is going on as reports from his family have varied. I am observer. An unmediated glimpse is required.

I don't want to alert anyone to anything so I am going to sit tight in the Taurus. I could ask there, through that door marked OFFICE, for one Joshua Brian Coffey, but I think not. Instead, I enjoy an entire 1948 live concert at Carnegie Hall including this revelation—the vocalist Kay Davis— and then turn to commercial radio and hear the ravings of sports talk from Chicago, which includes the flaying of a Bears quarterback, as usual. And in a break in the rain—a rent in the girdle?—I approach the cigarette machine right outside the OFFICE entrance and pump bills in until the push of a button drops a pack of Marlboro Lights to the bottom slot. I slip into the office because I can see a bowlful of Red Rock matchbooks just inside and enjoy for the moment the entelechy of the Red Rock design, convenient access to amenities, parking, matches, smokes, soda and snack machines; and a bed. I navigate a few runnels of water headed for drains in the parking lot to get back to my Taurus. I can sit as stubbornly in my car as my son has proved to be, though he escaped the sign by eight days. Did he? And I can smoke. But no, I'll give them to my son. He's a Gemini.

O entelechy, the internal perfecting principle, form of forms,
of the Red Rock Inn.

○ ○ ○ ○ ○

Taking stock in where we are, where I am, in middle America
at the very end of historical time,
heaven and the earth.
without form, void
darkness upon the face of the deep.
Light. Day and Night
Some confusion about what the firmament divides.
Call it Heaven. And the evenings and the mornings
Seas, grass, herb. Seed, fruit

Day and night again.
Seasons. Heaven, yea, and Earth.
Stars.
First, the whales, then every winged fowl
And the cattle and the creeping things and then man.

Let us make a man, a boy and a girl.
Let them have dominion
over the fish over the fowl over the cattle over every living thing
    that creepeth
Over all the earth

Fruitful! Multiply! Replenish!
Subdue the earth

Alexa, what does the Indiana state seal symbolize?

Alexa: The current design, first made in 1816, was not officially adopted until 1963. It depicts a woodsman chopping trees while a bison flees in the foreground, symbolizing the advance of settlement on the American frontier. The sun sets over hills in the background.

The sun has set. Over hills. Now in the foreground.

My son is no longer wandering in the woods. Nor is he the bison fleeing the woodsman. He is humbly fighting to remain sober and free and alive in settled America. No more errands, no more wilderness. He's in a Red Rock Inn. At this second.

∘ ∘ ∘ ∘ ∘

It's the stutter in American literature that interests me. I hear the stutter as a sounding of uncertainty. What is silence or not quite silenced [as in Billy Budd]. . . . *A return is necessary, a way for women to go. Because we are in the stutter. We were expelled from the Garden of the Mythology of the American Frontier. The drama's done. We are the wilderness. We have come onto the stage stuttering.*

> —Howe to Ed Foster, *Talisman* interview, reprinted in *Birth-mark*, Wesleyan University Press, 1992, p. 181

What Howe knew of her father Mark DeWolfe Howe, the brilliant Harvard constitutional scholar, biographer, friend (and colleague) to F. O. Matthiessen and Perry Miller, themselves very prominent scholars on Puritan New England, was that he, like his friends, like his colleagues, excluded women from their professional purview. This both pained Susan Howe and has sustained her brilliant analyses of colonial New England's ills and injustices as well as their grip on today. Perhaps the most enlightening essay I have found on Howe's poetics, oddly enough, is in the *Yale Journal of Law and Feminism*, written by law professor Marie Ashe. In order to revisit and freshly interpret a dated but foundational work, *Nomos and Narrative*, by one Robert M. Cover, whose "intellectual father" was Mark DeWolfe Howe, Ashe deconstructs both men's work, this "father and son" duo, and, with tremendous panache and insight, using Susan Howe texts to do so—father and daughter, as it were.

" 'Harvard was very privileged during the forties and fifties, so male,' Susan told Ed Foster in the revealing *Talisman* interview. 'The Matthiessen book [F. O. Matthiessen, *American Renaissance: Art and Expression in the Age of Emerson and Whitman*]: an intellectual and poetic Renaissance minus Emily Dickinson. Minus Harriet Beecher Stowe. Minus Margaret Fuller. Of course, minus Frederick Douglass as well. Women weren't the only ones subtracted. . . . I can't quite so simply say I grew up in a false community—a community that fancied itself as liberal. . . . But you see, it *was* false if you were a girl or a woman who was not content to be considered second-rate.' "

What Ashe gets so right is owing to her attunement to Howe's fierce brand of feminism and its place deep in the structure of her work—and its dissent from her father's. Ashe quotes Rachel Blau du Plessis to great effect; the poet and astute critic had characterized Howe's project as "an astonishing self-portrait of an artist, a woman, trying to inherit herself, to work herself into her own—'patrimony'? 'anarchy'? No, into her own liberty."

Inherit herself. To be both parent and child, dissolving mysteries.

o o o o o

Often, in the street, the young children of strangers pull up and look at me; they will incline their head toward their father's thigh, or paw absently for their mother's hand and eye me, curiously; they actually stop, sometimes with a shy smile, as if we are suddenly sharing a joke or an intimacy or something slightly embarrassing that we'd both forgotten. The parents look around and then look at me, warmly, warmly. As well, infants sunk in strollers or prams, as I approach them in my stride from the opposite direction, catch my eye and lock in for the few seconds until their conveyance passes me and I them. I never see them again. I never see any of them again. But I keep seeing something of them, and they see something of me. What is this? It is as if the leaves indeed are full of children *who see me*. Do they recognize me—as a kindred spirit, a potential playmate under review, a standby protector? Or do I pose a threat? Am I completely misreading these situations? Am I in the leaves with the children? Am I a foundling unfound, or hiding, or lost? Am I here by choice? Do I love it? Need it? Both? Am I riffling the pages of artists looking for someone, or a place to hide? Looking for the children? Perhaps they are laughing. Eliot glossed his lines "the leaves were full of children" with the French "cache-cache," or hide-and-seek.

Last night in the deep night I put a paragraph in and took a paragraph out, put a paragraph in and took a paragraph out, took it out and made a change and put the paragraph back in and saw a change that needed to be made and took the paragraph out again, never the same paragraph in and out because of this but the same paragraph in, and out, because of that. Then this morning, in the thin light, I write a paragraph down, put it in.

PART II
The Stacks

Death worship, her Emily—not mine—violence eroticized in an insular place, the inevitable held off and held off till release, total and irrevocable once there and onto of course the unknown and unknowable,

> *Past the Houses,*
> *Past the Headlands,*
> *Into deep Eternity—*

Wrapped up in lace and pins she left it all—"Called home," Emily Dickinson wrote in her life's last communication (to her cousins)—no longer the loaded gun on duty in a corner but a corpse, finally out of the House on Main Street, borne in her casket to the cemetery by the Irish laborers she requested. She had indeed stopped for Death, her first and only surrender. She "crossed her father's ground" now that she had no Will.

The seventh sentence of Susan Howe's magnificent *My Emily Dickinson* reads thus: "The ambiguous paths of kinship pull me in opposite ways at once." The keening and anger, the torrent of insights that flash through, page after page, at times are trance-like.

> *Killdeer is a hunter's gun. Together We will hunt and kill for pleasure. American frontiersmen were generally men on the make. Land in the West was a commodity to be exploited for profit just as land in the East had been. The Civil War will or will not expiate Our Sin. During the first two Removes of Emily Killdoe's Captivity Narrative of Discovery; the unmentioned sun, blazing its mythopoetic kinship with Sovreign and shooting its rhyme,—flash of sympathy with Gun, has been steadily declining. Dickinson, an unwed American citizen with "—son" set forever in her name, sees God cooly from the dark side of noon.*
> —from Howe, *My Emily Dickinson*, p. 94

What is Howe hearing here from whatever noon? This is so condensed that little light emerges, unlike Dickinson's poems, with their atomized and abstracted emissions into flashing air and letters and dashes, with metaphors that still stun—a woman's life as a loaded gun waiting to be fired—and in which meaning spills into bright if elusive possibilities, "as Lightning on a Landscape / Exhibits Sheets of Place—"

The "ambiguous kinship" Howe references in this instance is her mixed feelings about William Carlos Williams's apparent dismissal of Dickinson's poetry that Howe, however, reads differently (though she does not say how). In any event, the uncertainty buoys her, sets her afloat, as if on a winding river, like Thoreau's Concord River, she says, headed, she says, at the end of her one-page introduction, "toward certain discoveries."

I cannot help but suspect willful attempts at misdirection in much of the critical work on Howe. Take Marjorie Perloff, the Stanford standard-bearer of critical excellence and daring when it comes to the American avant-garde. In her 1989 essay on Howe, " 'Collision or Collusion with History': Susan Howe's Articulation of Sound Forms in Time," collected in her *Poetic License* (1990), Perloff herself both colludes and collides with the Howe story, asserting, so controvertibly, that she "know[s] of no Howe poem that is directly autobiographical or personal"; she will admit only to the presence of "emotive" qualities in the poems. But Perloff has somehow unknowing known that the Howe she is studying—the cool, radical chronicler of a poetic tradition born in prophecy, bled into the soil she was born to, alert and keen to the ghosts of Gloucester and New Bedford, New Haven, Northampton and Plymouth and Deerfield, Turner Falls and Hadley, transfixed and appalled at the treatment of First Peoples and white females, who makes so much of a single river of an Algonkian name that bifurcates a state, maps over maps—will become the Howe whose line lengthens into tales of her mother, her mother's Ireland, her father's study, her younger sister, her own little girl's dreams, a young woman's ambitions and doubts, her marriages, deaths of spouses, love of children. She wrote of her father in one of her earliest books, *The Secret History of the Dividing Line*, her father's first name the first word in the poem— "mark mar ha forest"—amply spaced on the page and prefaced in her introductory remarks at a public reading in 1978 with "My father's name was Mark, and my son's name is Mark," so what is Perloff's blind spot? I cannot judge.

Other critical assessments of Howe's work see the relation of her work to her life differently. Increasingly commonplace are writers on Howe avidly contending with her engagements with early colonial American history and literature. Poet Stephen Collis is one who effectively connects the obvious dots. In his study *Through the Words of Others: Susan Howe and Anarcho-Scholasticism*, he sifts through the poet's affiliations of influence—James Clarence Mangan and Melville, Melville and Hawthorne, Dickinson and Shakespeare, Olson and Shakespeare, Olson and Dickinson, and Howe and all of them. "They have all lost their fathers," Collis writes. "Parent-predecessors attract them to their futures as writers." Or as Howe herself states it in her prose piece "Marginalia," "I thought one way to write about a loved author would be to follow what trails he followed through words of others." Or in the poem "Frame"—

> *ere I were*
> *wher*
>
> *father father*
> *O it is the old old*
> *myth*

"Through the words of others," concludes Collis, "they seek lost origins."

This seems to me the central fact of Howe's work, this consistent insistence upon a "presence of absence," that something or someone is missing. It is, for me, the key to her work's obliquity, its hidden measures and missing parts, its torn and rent surfaces, a kind of violence committed to the text as if it were the shroud of an ancestor who is despised because gone and prized in equal measure for its trace or shadow still. A MARK.

Is this Mark the father who died suddenly mid-career when Susan Howe was thirty, or the "Mark," again in *The Secret History of the Dividing Line*,

> *hidden from our vision*
> *MARK*
> *border*
> *bulwark. an object set up to indicate a boundary or position*
> *hence a sign or token*
> *impression of trace*

Is this the secret, is this the history, is this the dividing line?

Go, said the bird.

This scene, wrote Derrida (as quoted in Howe's essay "Encloser" from *The Politics of Poetic Form*, ed. by Charles Bernstein, p. 192), *has never been read for what it is, for what is at once sheltered and exposed in its metaphors. It is all about fathers and sons, about bastards unaided by public assistance, about glorious legitimate sons, about inheritance, sperm, sterility. Nothing is said of the mother, but this will not be held against us. And if you look hard enough as in those pictures in*

which a second picture can be made out, one might be able to
discern her unstable form, drawn upside-down in the foliage at
the back of the garden.

Howe's engagement with this quotation from Derrida's
"Plato's Pharmacy" reads,

"What if the faintly drawn second picture at the back
of the garden suddenly tells the scene for what it is? . . . The
past is present. We are all part of the background."

And she breaks into verse at the end of the three-page essay:

> *Turned back from turning back*
> *as if a loved country*
> *faced away from the traveler*
> *No pledged premeditated daughter*
> *no cold cold sorrow no barrier.*

ooooo

I sit now in a town above a lake in upstate New York where
Howe had a residency in 1987 and wrote a text, *Thorow*, a
"child of the Adirondacks / taking notes like a spy," and she
is not talking about me, though she could be. Ironically,
at that same time I was writing poems in Hatfield, Mass.,
plotting an escape in a farmhouse on the western bank of the
Connecticut River, across from Hadley, both towns Puritan
settlements of Indian lands, rich with loam and human
blood. I spent most of a day and part of an evening that year,
walking the river flats, from the end of the potato fields
behind our rented farmhouse, along the edge of the nearly

still river, walked downstream all the way to Canary Island. I swam and waded and napped and sunned myself in naked fashion, finishing my tour back at a Hatfield tavern and there decided to leave my second wife, Brenda. The poem I was working on then—poems clipped and extracted in parts and ordered from Gertrude Stein's lectures in America—

> *Nothing*
> *makes nothing*
> *makes any difference*
> *if the*
> *same*
> *person talking*
> *and the listening*
> *does the talking and the listening*

—sustained me. I did not know Susan Howe from Helen Adam at the time; yet one day she and I would share a publisher.

What did Howe find in my Adirondacks as I prepared to leave her New England? Hard to say what she found, but what she brought was an edged arrogance that is perhaps a necessity to interlopers in this wild, this wilderness, as real and raw today as Concord was in Thoreau's time or even John Cotton's. Perhaps Howe, at fifty years of age and mother of two at the time, survivor of two marriages, saw Lake George and "the shores of history" as a wilderness in need of taming. The lake, she wrote in her introduction, "was a blade of ice to write across not knowing what She." The mysterious, unstated fate of the subject-object *She* is indeed the not to know. The She—not her, *she*!—"[goes] down to unknown regions of indifferentiation [*sic*]. The Adirondacks," she writes, "occupied me," imagining her own captivity. Like Thoreau, she considers naming things, staking out her wilderness with her words, like any poet, marauder, reformer, settler. Was Anne Hutchinson slaughtered in Rananchqua, so-called by the Lenape (the Delawares), or in New Netherland, or in the Bronck of the Swedish settler Jonas Bronck, or simply The Bronx? Or was it Pelham? In any event, Hutchinson was brutally slain, along with all but one of her children, a daughter, on the banks of a river that now bears She, no Her, name. And the questions of language—what words mean to whom—bob and swirl and dive and melt.

Howe's *Thorow* opens:

> Go on the Scout they say
> They will go near Swegachey
>
> I have snow shoes and Indian shoes
>
> Idea of my present
> not my silence

And She is already lost, 100 miles to the northwest, but the first of *Thorow*'s magnificent strides, as if, beyond the western border of New England, the poet is eating up ground, from Bolton Landing to Fort Stanwix (in Rome, NY) to the Great Lakes to "the German Flatts" in

Herkimer, "scribbling the ineffable," she circumscribes in her wild ramble the Adirondack Park's six million square acres, "Author the real author / acting the part of a scout." Lost, almost, but it would seem ecstatically, following an Irishman, "the real author" Howe calls him, William Johnson, as he surveys his trading options with the Six Nations, becoming wealthy and lionized by both sides, across borders, by the British and the Iroquois Confederacy. By one account Howe is reading the fourteen volumes of Johnson's papers at the New York State Library in Albany.

Long walks the poet takes on her own, too, giant steps again, bravely forth—Erebus, Shelving Rock, summits and outcrops on the east side of the lake—named George after the king by Johnson, an Irish Catholic who for expediency's sake converted to the Church of England and came to the foot of the 32-mile body of water to command the British and Native American forces against the French.

"A sort of border life," Howe writes. Cross waters, oceans, rivers, lakes, where men move along surfaces (at their peril). Perhaps Howe's lake of ice *is* to be etched upon, whether by boot or blade or stylus. Or blood. Red blood in the white ice I once saw one winter years ago, someone's bloody nose, drops, like the thin, dark red bingo chips provided during Bingo Night at Church of the Assumption, Redford, NY. The blood of Christ. Game of chance.

"If they look alike and are not sisters. All at once. Dove and dove-tail." This quotation is taken from one of Gertrude

Stein's "Sentences" carnets, or little notebooks; it appears in Howe's beautiful *Spontaneous Particulars: The Telepathy of Archives* from Christine Burgin's imprint at New Directions, a book that might serve as the Susan Howe mission statement as it is a distillation of her aesthetic, her practice, her belief. The Stein quotation and many other citations in her book are fruits of her roaming in the stacks at the Sterling Library at Yale, Howe's sacred chapel, or in her words (which end the book)—

> *The inward ardor I feel while working in research libraries is intuitive. It's a sense of self-identification and trust, or the granting of grace in an ordinary room, in a secular time.*
> —Howe

A secular *chapel.*

The "factual telepathy of poetry": Howe often speaks of it. If she is the sender I am the receiver of whatever she is in receipt of. If they are sisters and do not look alike. . . . Dovetail and dove. I have no brother do I. Beckett felt he had a twin within. If I am no one else am I incomplete?

Life is dialogic, said Bakhtin. A shared event; a transtextuality. To have lived is not enough, they have to talk about it, said Estragon. *Have to. Will.*

There may be twins everywhere if we could see them.

o o o o o

Mary Manning, Susan Howe's mother, was a year older than Samuel Beckett, Mary born in 1905, Sam in 1906. They grew up in Dublin as upper-middle-class Irish Protestants and fading gentry. They endured the Easter Rising, the War of Independence, the Civil War, and the founding of the Free State—along with the First World War, during which monarchies of several kinds were dissolved. In Dublin, fatefully, they were close to where an anachronistic/specious Celtic Revival was taking place every season in the public theaters, and Yeats was writing his plays and poems. Mary's mother, named Susan, was close friends from youth with Bill Beckett, Sam's father. In a curious twist, each, early on, when single, was besotted with a member of the same well-to-do Catholic family, the Murphys, whose patriarch forbade any possible linkage of a Murphy to either of the two Protestant families. Neither Susan Bennett, who fancied a Murphy son, nor William Beckett, who fancied Eva Murphy, ever got over their losses, according to Mary Manning. Eventually, each did wed, Susan Bennett to John Manning and William Beckett to May Roe. Bill and Susan remained very close, and, according to Mary, the two would occasionally take drives in Bill's car to commiserate about the loves they were not allowed. On at least one occasion, they took little Mary along in the backseat; many decades later Mary would relate the tale to Beckett's biographer James Knowlson. Some scholars have speculated that Beckett wondered who he would have been or become if his father had married into the Murphys, rather than into the wealthy grain merchant Roe family, whose daughter May (Mary) was basically a Christian fundamentalist. Was Beckett's "twin" a Beckett-Murphy in some unrealized realm of the possible? As any Beckett scholar knows, the names Murphy and May and Mary and even Eva swirl through his texts. These speculations are considered fair game.

As here, in *Footfalls*, V (Voice) to M (May): "I say the floor here, now bare, this strip of floor, once was carpeted, a deep pile. Till one night, while still little more than a child, she called her mother and said, Mother, this is not enough. The mother: Not enough? May—the child's given name—May: Not enough. The mother: What do you mean, May, not enough, what can you possibly mean, May, not enough? May: I mean, Mother, that I must hear the feet, however faint they fall. The mother: The motion alone is not enough? May: No, Mother, the motion alone is not enough, I must hear the feet, however faint they fall. [May resumes pacing.]"

Traces. One wants things to remember. Even footfalls.

The short play ends. "Mother. Will you never have done? Will you never have done . . . revolving it all. It? It all. In your poor mind. It all. It all."

"Premeditated daughter?"

"Pledged?"

∘ ∘ ∘ ∘ ∘

I wake this morning to this morning's text message:

You were right about her. You were right about everything. I
wanted to believe that we were in love and that that was all that
mattered. But she betrayed me. And fucked me over in such an
intense way there is no turning back. Dad I am so sorry that we
grew apart. I never wanted that. But I cant expect you to put up
with the life and times of a junkie. I walked 30 miles. And my feet
are solid blisters. I tried to get to the girls but it was too far. Its
over. Im kicked out pennyless and ruined. I just wanted someone
to know that she destroyed me. She laughed in my foolish face.
Tonight I slide into the st joe river and breath as deep as I can. Im
so sorry. I love you dad. Im really going through some shit I think
im ok im sorry.
Ah well we pick up the stones we want. And carry them forever. I
love you dad.

I just cant get it together. Im a degenerate gambler. A junkie. A
liar, a terrible husband a terrible father. Im just about the worst
human being on the planet. Oh yea. Terrible son. She and I just
cant make it. We simplu added gambling to our list of addictions.
It seems like something just flipped in my brain and now im easily
strung out on everything. I dont even understand it. Im alone out
of money homeless. This is all too familiar. Im just a fucking waste.
Dad I know that you will hate to hear this but it think im going to
take her with me. She wrecked my house arrest two days before
reporting. That almost guarantees jail for me. And im sorry I just
cant let it go.

Let it go dad says.

Peculiar, how scars shine, wrote the poet Gregory Orr, who was saved walking these Bolton Landing fields I look at today.

Hard here to fathom what to do. House arrest now.

Now, in a relatively sunny isle, a watery death in the St. Joseph river is averted.

Dad, can you order me a pizza?

Last night seen. No nothing. Emptiness itself, broom clean so that remainder only containment. Have to end somewhere. Empty me. I have done.

At last perhaps. See it that way. Try. At last, on empty, on words I know of I am full though have had my last. Attrition now. The same thing, as addition. Can't be, only in fancy. I fancy. Here we are.

Once, several onces. It was emptiness that drove the charge or need, *mon besoin, mon faim*. Not now, nothing doing. No spinning old stories into tales or worrying words into being up at night going through drawers, becoming, ungirdling. Roaring. No. I've come to my last . . . Him. Or me.

I find some solace in the easy chair of the infinitive:

to be

to have

to do

to say

to go
to get
to make
to know
to think

to take

to slow down

to see
to want
to look
to use

to find

to give

to work
to call
to try
to ask
to need
to feel
to become

to leave
to mean
to keep
to let
to begin

to seem

to begin to seem

to help

to talk

to start
to show
to hear
to play
to move
to like
to live
to believe

to hold

to happen

to remain
to write
to provide

to sit
to stand
to lose
to pay
to include
to continue
to learn
to change
to lead
to understand
to watch
to follow

to stop

to create

to speak

to read

to allow

to add

to grow
to open

to walk

to win

to offer
to remember
to remember to love

to consider
to appear

to wait
to serve

to die

to send
to expect
to build

to stay
to fall
to reach

to kill
to suggest
to raise

to pass

to report

to decide

This illusion of agency welcome enough.

○ ○ ○ ○ ○

As a child, Beckett would bring home stones from the sea and build nests for them, in the crooks of trees, meant to protect the stones from the sea. *I took advantage of being at the seaside to put in a store of sucking stones.* The stones, the stones. The words.

My son with the gun loves stones. Today he texts me that he has beaten the last charge over his head—that he pointed a gun at his methedrine-addicted lady friend now avowed enemy. The charge was dismissed. Now to come out of the woods and into the world.

C'mon boy.

○ ○ ○ ○ ○

A fresh look at Howe's work is by British academic Will
Montgomery. His *Poetry of Susan Howe: History, Theology,
Authority* from 2010 manages to lift Howe the poet clear of
the cloudy morass of the L=A=N=G=U=A=G=E school, which
has served perhaps unwittingly to give Howe cover and which
cover Howe has, perhaps reluctantly, perhaps not unwittingly,
taken. Cover from what? I don't know—lack of community,
the cold perch of her singular genius, perhaps. Montgomery
acknowledges and indeed probes Howe's place in, shall we say,
the American grain—Olson, Williams, Stevens—and cites
her study of the religious rhetoric and narratives of colonial
New England—John Cotton, Cotton Mather, Jonathan
Edwards, and most notably the antinomian heretic Anne
Hutchinson, placing Hutchinson at the head of a succession of
Americans operating throughout the long period as witnesses
on the New Jerusalem soil: in such company as Hawthorne,
Melville, Whitman, and of course Emily Dickinson.
Montgomery does not, however, traffic much in the 20th-
century commentaries of Charles Bernstein, Bruce Andrews,
and Lynn Hejinian, who tend in various ways to align Howe's
practice with the tenets of the L=A=N=G=U=A=G=E group—
"resistance to syntactical/logical closure," "radical language
practice, a practice constitutive of a shift from 'written'
to 'writing' "; etc. That is, Howe's work, in Montgomery, is
seen through the L=A=N=G=U=A=G=E lens abstractly as
something entirely disruptive in its intent on the level of
language production, which hardly squares with the deeply
embedded historical specificity of Howe's subject matter and
focus—she is recorrecting, recuperating, and resurrecting
historical language, not atomizing it. She is not interested
in the Steve McCaffery assertion that language is always

playing a "theologicolinguistic trick" on the unenlightened
reader by assuming language as a window onto a (false)
(capitalist) reality. For Howe, that very much *is* what she
finds in the language of archives—not a way to a "new
real" (Bernstein) but to an old real that is still with us.
Language for Howe is not all materiality, soundscapes, and
orthography raining anew on those in the know; it is/can be
telepathy, indeed a medium of transmission. She has said
somewhere she doesn't agree with the L=A=N=G=U=A=G=E
poets one bit, though out of their loose association, each has
learned something from the other.

". . . the presence of antinomianism in [Howe's] work can be
better understood as the result of an anxiety about origins
that causes her to fashion a particular literary genealogy
around her own preoccupations. Like many other writers
before her, she implicitly writes herself into her own strong
reading of literary history."—Will Montgomery

Indeed she does, and she believes that even today, those of
the antinomian spirit, that is, people anti-*nomos*, anti-law,
-scripture, -rules, -tradition—are the true poets. If anything,
this is where her transit intersects with an element of
America's onetime poetic avant-garde.

Anne Hutchinson is Howe's hero, make no mistake. Not
Emerson, not Whitman, not Edwards or Melville or Olson
or Stevens (though Stevens seems the most dear to her—she
even got into his longtime home, like a spy, she hinted in a
reading, at 18 Westerly Terrace in Hartford).

From *The Difficulties*:
interview with Janet Ruth Falon:

Q: Your father was American?
HOWE: He certainly was. After the war was over he never once went back to Europe. He never went with us to Ireland. He hardly ever left Cambridge.

Q: I'm sensing that you've come to some kind of resolution about your American split, and the Emily Dickinson [book] has perhaps brought an end to this branch of your concern and you're at the beginning of new work. Is that true for your work, that there's something you have to work out, you get to a conclusion, and you're done and you move on?
HOWE: Yes.

Q: Do you sense what the next branch is?
HOWE: I'm working on a new series of poems. A lot of my writing I did in Ireland or I did here, thinking of Ireland and it's a split. It's not only that I break words and phrases, but the works are split. Right now [1986] I'm writing work I would consider American. Most people don't think of their writing in such a weird way, but it's what I do.

Q: Is there a sadness in the loss of this conflict now that it's finally resolved?
HOWE: I don't think conflicts are ever dissolved. You just learn to abide them.

". . . loss of this conflict"; what conflict? ". . . finally resolved?" Howe: Not ever. You live with them. Abide with thee.

Howe's audacious act of historical appropriation, a kind of reenactment of a North American land grab justified by a Puritan belief in the absolute right of the members of the Elect to have sovereignty (Howe seems pleased to refer to it as "suivrnty veragnit") over every living thing, is a project steeped in tales of brutality and acts of violence preserved in the most exclusive precincts of North American story and sign—research libraries. And researched extensively, it can be said, by not only her father, Mark DeWolfe Howe, but his Harvard colleague and frequent houseguest Perry Miller, whose foundational study of Puritan political doctrine, *Errand into the Wilderness*, is dedicated to Mark and Molly Howe.

Historical violence as textual presence—even human presence, then, for Howe, who with her sister Fanny, as teenagers, endured many a dinner party at their home thronged with the Harvard elite who had professions staked on understanding and rationalizing what their forebears had done.

Charles Olson once said, "We were the last First People," by virtue of the poetic sympathy for the guilty colonizer I can only conclude. Call me Ishmael or do you mean Ahab?

Unseen, Howe is able to ransack the stacks of lost or forgotten testimony and emerge with her own works superbly produced and published that, while leading the reader to bizarre and at first obscure scenes of sociohistorical and even religious conflict, almost transcendent in levels of violence and suffering, remind us that this is still an America increasingly recognizable today.

Howe has brought us talismans, like scalps, dried, wrapped in spruce root, ceremonial—insane objects. We lay them out and try to read them.

In the 1980s, Howe's mid-career intensity was trained upon the work of the poet Charles Olson (1910–1970). Her correspondence with Olson scholar George Butterick is rich with confession, not of sins but of specific literary infatuations and an overall anxiety not so much of origins but of influence. The engagement with Olson's work seems to stoke a fire in which it is easy to see the image of Herman Melville dancing, but perhaps father figures as well, for Olson himself was wrestling with his father as well as cultural fathers (Ezra Pound first among them). Olson indulged himself in these reveries and leapt and danced himself—and projected an aesthetic into some geometric and geographic space like an ever-arriving conquistador trashing maps, huffing and puffing, smoking and wearing out women, his prose and poems percussing and booming like six-stroke engines, lines and phrases torqued, knotted and unknotted in some kind of fierce manic action that indeed, at the very least, took up a lot of SPACE. In a book. His intense engagement with Melville and Melville's with Shakespeare is truly contagious, telepathy as contagion perhaps. Howe caught it. Like Olson, she has a poem titled "We were the last First People."

ooooo

Dad I really would like to get out
If here.
 A guy just pulled a gun on

me. Aske me who I was
gonna be jumping. Said e
heard what I was saying...
  Never said anything,
never even seen the guy
before in m life.

Then get out; bad section
of S Bend yr aunt implied.

Well Dad that's not easily
done. I'm sort of stying
rent free in a house. The
only obligytion I have it to
do the remodel. There are
not many other options.
But believe me. It's fucking
terrible. And dangerous.
What am I upposed to
do.?

I walked the gun down to
the barrel touched my
face. He
was bluffing.

With thoughts of Oliver Cromwell, for some reason, Puritan
enforcer. There is a Cromwell, Connecticut, named after
the Lord Protector of the Commonwealth of England, who

reduced to obedience Catholic Ireland, seeing to the deaths of 40 percent of the population.

From Cromwell, 10th September 1649, to Sir Arthur Aston, governor of the town of Drogheda:

> Sir, having brought the army of the Parliament of
> England before this place, to reduce it to obedience,
> I thought it fit to summon you to deliver the same into
> my hands to their use. If this be refused, you will
> have no cause to blame me. I expect your answer
> and remain your servant,
> O. Cromwell.

Two days later, after Cromwell's brutal siege of Drogheda:

> For the Chief Officer commanding in Dundalk.
> Drogheda, 12th September 1649.
>
> Sir, I offered mercy to the Garrison of Drogheda, in
> sending the Governor a Summons before I attempted
> the taking of it. Which being refused brought their
> evil upon them.
>   If you, being warned thereby, shall surrender your
> Garrison to the use of the Parliament of England,
> which by this I summon you to do, you may thereby
> prevent effusion of blood. If, upon refusing this Offer,
> that which you like not befalls you, you will know
> whom to blame.
> I rest,
> Your servant,
> O. Cromwell.

The complacency of much American poetry, I can think of few exceptions, assumes the givens of not only place but space. The audacity of Thoreau, his "Walking," an educated man with friends at Harvard and an accommodating mother, traces the savage in the wild and names it, the poet as nominator, like Adam, like Cromwell. Or Olson, who thought he was "turn[ing] time into . . . space & its live air," which only sculptors and dancers do. Making and remaking worlds (time, space, the whole of dominion) in their own image in their own minds for their own masters now no longer possible even viable even decent. The world is disappearing if you think it is, and we do, I do, it is obvious, but it is really only lingering, absorbing all the matter and carbon we have extracted in order to hasten our already blip-blip of demise, enduring us with a shrug, a shrug indeed. The world is disappearing as to the blind I suppose, certainly to the dying. "But the clouds in the sky," wrote Yeats in one of his last poems, "when the horizon fades"—that, and a bird's sleepy cry are the final fleeting things we see, hear, fading to black, and to silence. Yeats's greatest lines, said Beckett, who made a television play out of them, admirably resisting the weakening dark while honoring it.

Just got pistol whipped
and pockets ran.. never
saw the guys. Woke up to
getting whacked. This

place is a war zone. I'm ok
though.
Believe it or not crack has
returned. That and the
new drug toon. It's got
the city on fire.

Now he sits somewhere on a fall Saturday, his younger half
brother has been found dead, and he—my son—is distraught
and high or drunk or just *very* distraught, murmuring
beneath a certain threshold of communicability. I think he
said this, I think he said that; I think he knows this, or that,
or nothing. He texts:

This can't be right
Fucking Jason
He will turn up
That's my brother. I love
Jason.

On the phone he seems unsure that his brother is dead;
perhaps just missing. He says the whole family has hated on
Jason for years. He says he has too. I remind him he's been
incarcerated for many years, and that, years before that,
when he was free, and with a home, he put his brother up in a
hospital bed in his own living room while he recovered from
several lower-body bone fractures. Somehow Jason managed
to get himself accused of stealing money when no one was
looking. Fucking Jason. He was an addict, a skateboarder, a
cartooner hobbyist. I think he has a twelve-year-old son.

Now to Josh, now out, now in, now back out, now me to him: somehow on, no how on. Maybe it will amuse him, deliver him from his suffering. For a paragraph or two.

No.

Not your story but find your story.

∘ ∘ ∘ ∘ ∘

How about I tell you about Howe, about how I got to here, on the issue of Howe, Susan, *the poetry of Howe*, let me have that phrase—*the poetry of Howe*—as *the city of Savannah* served for Gertrude Stein, when it meant not at all the literal Georgia (U.S.) city, but a ship, a ship in (literally) her 1916 work *Mexico*, a limpid, tender, charming play not about the country but only the words and sounds themselves; grant me *the poetry of Howe* as a place like that, that has "poetry" in it, owned by and credited to an author, her assemblage of English words (mostly) and in her own format and style (with the collaboration of designers, archivists, and publishers), into which I have wandered. Think of it as Mexico but with me in it, or the ship the *City of Savannah* with me on it. Whether I am an illegal immigrant, a stowaway, a paying tourist, or a reader in or on the poetry of Susan Howe, my right to be there is in being there, at the very least and it is a valid claim. By my lights. By your lights. Maybe you will get to Mexico, son. To Matamoros, where your mother was from.

How I see Howe is about how I see, and how I see is unavoidably rooted in who I am, me, who could not possibly

99

even theoretically see how I see from another person,
that is, to be rooted in one, though the attempt to do so
is at the heart of civility and religion and conscience and
some narrative art, but so sited in—and often cited for—
plagiarism, possession, fraud. But I am no criminal, son, I
didn't mean this life for you and I could not save you, it is
clear. How I see Howe, then, is repetitive, in that I am seeing
from who I am. Or iterative. Perhaps. I don't know, but I
will say this: I believe that Howe, *I suspect* that Howe, is like
the child who had painfully to choose one parent to favor in
the aftermath of divorce, and that Howe chose to favor her
Yankee father, and not the Irish father who was so far away,
and not even in her beloved Ireland but in Paris. A quarter
century after Mark DeWolfe Howe's early death we are told
that he was indeed in forensic fact Susan Howe's birth father,
she being heir to a still-ascendant North American colonial
patrimony and not to a doomed Anglo-Irish merchant class
with a Nobel laureate in it. I am not saying I see here my life
only that my life sees it.

How did Howe choose to favor the Yankee father? All I know
is her work.

At a point far down the road the Howe and Beckett tracks
meet, at a vanishing point of sorts, an abstract junction
of two historical bodies of work, two writers with much
in common and much in mystery. What they come to are
deep analyses of inherited traditions. Howe's is the Puritan
tradition of her father, Mark DeWolfe Howe, his forebears,

and the rebel antinomian dissent, while Beckett's is the scholastic tradition central to his basically 19th-century education—that is, the Greeks. Still, the works of both artists can partially be understood at levels close to a recognizable surface—as engaged scholar-artists, uninterested in current trends or contemporary issues, exploring liturgical rebellion on the one hand and its implications for artistic ethics (Howe) and scholastic philosophy on the other (Beckett), where the predominance of reason carries the day and is forever proven inadequate. That's one of the levels at which these two artists operate, working with two ultimately (if dissimilar) Christian traditions. I admit there is something unsatisfying about this, too reductive, too dismissive of the mysteries and oppositions that pock their creations. There may well be other parties and persuasions discernible in the shrubbery, the foliage, the leaves. Surely there are. The stacks.

PART III
The Woods

Now this is some creepy woods at night.

Why are you in the woods?

Just took a walk

No more sleeping in the woods!! A good thing!

I saw some large birds. They were fearful of humans but I used a bit of urban cover to get close. Once I was among them they seemed completely perplexed.

There are wild flamingos in Florida....Try to get to Ybor City, section of Tampa, Cuban and old vestiges of the Trafficante mob. Hand-rolled cigars. Pool hall. At least 10 years ago...

I tried to send video

Failed. Maybe too long.

I don't sleep in the woods anymore.

We are near Orlando, me and Wayne. 7 days. Luxury resort. A nice bonus I would say.

Great! Enjoy.

I certainly will lol. Thanks

What's next after Fla?

Home. But I made my pitch here to move the operation in a different direction. I believe that what we should be doing is buying liquidated items from places like liquidation dot com. And then stocking a brick and mortar retail store as well as a constant online income through 3 selling platforms. Ebay, Amazon. And Marketplace. I think it went great. Wayne said we are going to be rich...which I lived to hear...but Wayne is already rich...but him richer and me rich, well I like the sound of that.
Now we will still incorporate the storage auctions and estate sales. But the liquidated products are huge business. Some experts peg the total percent of online sales that are returned at 40%—that's a huge number. Of that percent 25% are broke or defective. The rest are brand new. And it is within those parameters that we will begin to grow our fortune.

Bricks and mortar—where?

Cheap space in emptied malls

But empty ain't good, for a mall.

Thats the thing we will offer the goods at a liquidation store. Wayne already owns the building. Market it: you're recycling! It ain't only liquidation...

What do I know!

I really proved my worth on this trip. I have lied and conned people into believing I am an expert at antiques, collectables, and appraisals. I have lied and conned people into believing that I run a large business. In fact I've done both those things now for so Long that they aren't cons anymore.

Yes but how to market it.

I've formulated an idea but I've not put it on the table yet. I don't think the timing is right.

I can only suggest that you be careful. You probably have a small margin for error, which should be part of your risk assessment. I know you know that, but it is easy to forget at times.

True. That is good advice. The hard part is keeping attuned to the market value of your goods. The new IPhone is a valuable desired item. But what will its value be a year from now? What about when the next version hits....no doubt it will still have value but pinning down that number is what butters the bread. If they sell quickly at 50. Would they sell evenly at $70. Will they sell still slower at $80, at the same time the higher return becoming another quantity to calculate. Perhaps at $80....none sell. All of these possibilities must be weighed to know how much you are able to pay on the Initial liquidation skid of 500 IPhones.

I would say over all the margin for error is much larger than let's say....for someone who works with storage lockers and estate sales, and with liquidation sales if you are knowledgeable. There are many many times that doubling and trippling your investment is easy as pie. Where a retailer makes a ten percent gain across the board. We own several larg buildings that serve as overflow storage bought and paid for. Freeing us from the overhead of renting storage space. Another great advantage.

Last day in Florida. I Like Florida. But I hate Kissimmi. It is the single most rotten town I've ever been in. Everything is fenced and caged. Fake and cheap. A sour dishonest people. And the traffic is dangerous beyond belief. I saw three car accidents and two people die since I've been here. Horrible.

What was the business reason to be there, as opposed to somewhere else? Did it payoff?

Yes it did pay off. The business reason was to have a Location to offset the seasonal markets of the Midwest with yearround market. Housing is a consideration.
Hey, I need to talk about something. I Need your help. Wayne has agreed to help me. But I think it's a lot to ask either of you. A while back you had helped me with something. And you said to me that if you were going to give me support that you would have to see some progress. I guess I am not entirely certain what that means but I think that has happened. And there is one thing in my life that I just can't get done on my own.
This is it in a nutshell. To really move forward I have to get my license back. Wayne has agreed to pay for some maybe half if

you will help. He knows a lawyer I'm going to try and speak with him tomorrow. He will either take on the task or refer me. Then I'll know more. It's the last piece of my old problems. Once I'm rid of it. Our business will take off.

Let me know cost.

Ok. I will as soon as I know.. might be a referral to someone else. But I'm hoping a traffic lawyer will take it on as opposed to an immigration attorney. Much cheaper. Ok heading home!

Oh no!
Brokedown outside Knoxville

Bummer. Rough Halloween. Now what?

Working on it
There goes my first appointment with the lawyer....
LoL
Working on it..radiator hose busted. Put tape and water but when we went to turn it over battery was dead.

Got the vehicle going again. The radiator hose. The Appalachian mountains oppose our travel. But we persist.
Might try a place other side of knoxville
I'm about exhausted. Broke and tired lol. I have my money invested in 15 bags of golf clubs and other merchandise easy double up once I get situated.

Hotel probably a good idea; business expense. Hey, Knoxville!
Cormac McCarthy country, once. Suttree right?

Yeah. I get it now. No country for old men. lol

Back on the road?

Yeah we are in Indianapolis
I just thought I saw Jason
It's just heart breaking
I got some difficult news.
The toxicology report came back. Jason died of a mixture of
morphine and fentanyl. The last person with him was a guy I
know. The detective said that this fucker was under 24 hour
surveillance because a man had died at his home recently of an
overdose. His toxicology report matches Jasons
I don't even want to go back.
Jason beat up his wife's boyfriend a week before Jason died. And
that's correct. Nasty biz
I feel that I will find that this guy I know and the guy Jason beat up
are friends. And at that point. I don't know.

I just think, regardless, you shouldn't run the risk of settling a dead
brother's scores.
But I gave up preaching

I don't want to go to prison. I love my kids and have a life.. Jason
is dead. Nothing will change that.. if they killed him. I just don't
know.

I'm home

Have a good night. have you an email? A friend sent me some photos from 1979, Central Park, you me your mom. I am holding you aloft. His son in his arms, aloft. Remember that?

Here. Chetaco@gmail.com

Harold Brodkey. Do you have that book of mine?

I have nothing from those days. Any days.

Sorry.

When I was in kissimmi a huge white owl flew right over me. Very close. And inside the city. Several days later miles away. A giant white owl again showed himself. Again very close and still sunlight.
I couldn't help but think that it was Jason.. I cried his name out. But no one answered. That little kid took mom's death the hardest. I miss him Dad. I miss him terrible.

No ficking heat at this house great.
Man. I'm exhausted to deal with this shit right now. I am considering taking up residence down south or Arizona. This winter shit is for the birds.
Summer in Ariz is something else as well.

But get to the higher elevations, not so broiling. Sedona!

Thats where I want to go. But that's a little dreamy. I got to deal with things here first.

You can do it. In dreams begin responsibilities. Yeats said that.

Yes. I believe I can.

Narrow your battles.

I can't let that guy get away with killing Jason. That's impossible. Nor will I punish him because Jason fucked up. Jason overdosed by accident. A tragedy but an accident.

I agree, let it be. Move on.

If I find out otherwise. And it will get out I'm sure. Even then if I were to act i would have to wait over a year to avoid being immediately rounded up and convicted. So for now I will put that on the backburner.

Move on. You are finally free.

We are different Dad. I love you and my kids. But if they killed Jason they are gone. No matter the cost.
Heat problem #1 for today.
I got an electric heater put back.. I'll be alright for tonight.

Are you tucking kidding me. These photos are amazing. Who sent those. That's unbelievable.
Could you send those to Damon

I don't have his email. If you do you can forward

Something is wrong with my God darn phone. I just did a hard reset and it only made it worse.. I'll try.. I gotta junk this one I think

How's the phone?

Junk
I tried hard reset. Did zero. Just lost stuff I wanted. It's that phone repair place ever since I took it there is had problems.

Figure out a good NEW phone to get. I will pay for it and ship wherever you say.

What? That's great. My job depends on my phone heavily. Wayne is not involved on my end. Sometimes he is listening but not understanding.

Ok.

ooooo

He shows me pictures of them on the road, the car breakdown. An old Honda. His boss the "multimillionaire" with "lots of buildings" is a rough looking fella with a long twist of braid hanging from his chin and a pretty good gut, his wife or female companion a tough-looking woman, bleached hair, maybe tanned. Florida, after all. The three of them. He stares into the engine, steam spewing; she leans against the side of the vehicle in a short dress and high boots, a large pocketbook clutched under her elbow as she works at the world in her phone, perhaps summoning help. A friend told me "This sounds like *Jackie Brown*." I ask what? "The whole thing. That team."

I google the multimillionaire's name and business and he appears to be a mover and trash hauler with a truck. This ain't Hollywood. This is no sign on a hill in lights. This is underground. There are no maps for this. Just song, maybe. Maybe American songlines. *Invisible Republic.*

From what my son has described, his business is trying to buy and sell abandoned goods from foreclosed houses, estate sales, padlocked storage locker contents in arrears, once an unclaimed ship container off the docks at Burns Harbor (full of, it turns out, spoiled fireworks). His many buildings are there to hold the stuff, which could be pallets of used iPhones, or recycled sets of golf clubs, or collections of old (vintage) (rusted) tools. I summarize here, for the sake of sanity and awareness.

From Damon:

I seen Josh, down for Jason's funeral. I drove to Plymouth from Racine. He wanted me to pick him up. He had no ride to his own brother's funeral. So I went to that house—I mean, the yard had just all this shit sitting there, toilet bowls and tanks, a cement mixer all crusted up, coils of wire and hose and rope. Junk under a tarp sagging with rainwater, looked like old children's toys and sports equipment. Sunken couches, a kitchen table missing a leg.

And the house itself, the doors had no doorknobs. It was a dead abandoned house with the guts out front like a dressed deer.

He wasn't there when I got there—he was at the Goodwill down the road, getting a suit. His boss was there walking the perimeter. He told me, like, what the fuck do you want. His wife or whatever she was in the van with the passenger door open. A crack whore I'd say, chewing gum and smoking, the radio blaring Red Hot Chili Peppers.

○○○○○

Phone really helped.. it has been an immediate relief. If I knew how much of a difference it would make I would have made this a priority. Thank you so very much.

I set the itinerary for each day. Tomorrow I have Wayne going to Indy to look at a roofing job while I get dropped off at a house in south bend. Wayne will quote the job and make a materials list. I will begin picking a hoarders house. Pulling items of value from what others see as only a confusing pile of trash. .
At 11:00 I will call Wayne and send him to whatever auctions or estate sales I have already vetted for him in Indy. I will return home to meet one of our workers who I will put to work finishing some windows. Wayne will meet with one of our workers to begin the roofing job. Once that is underway I head back to picking the hoarders house. Wayne drives back from Indy. At 7:00 pm Wayne meets me at the hoarders house. We have a meeting and I tell him how much money can be safely spent on the items I have selected. And I go through the Indy purchases and pull immediate

sales to be posted in the morning. That is a day in the life of Che Taco. That's me, Che Taco.

What's a hoarder's house?

A person who has filled their home with so many items that it has become unmanageable. There are homes so filled with goods that the structural integrity becomes an issue. It is a symptom of a deeper mental illness.

They can be gold mines. And they can be nauseating. This guy's mother was the hoarder. She has passed but her hoard remains. He tried to post an ad on Facebook saying whole contents of house for sale. It was not a successful venture. It's overwhelming for anyone. Hundreds came and narry a dent was made. Tomorrow I will process the whole house. And make a huge profit. The trick is to at a glance determine if money can be made or not. Stay or go. Split second and keep moving. It's really very easy. Hey if you have an extra moment could you give Damon a call.

About what?

About those pictures. I think he wants to thank you. I think he just likes you dad.

I think I just set up a huge deal.

I turned a one man cleaning job into a whole home property and contents acquisition. If I pull this off it will be nothing short of miraculous.

Good luck.

Disaster no deal

Was long shot, no?

Yes. But disappointed....there was a family dispute
Another brother showed up. Big mess. Oh well I've got to get
my head together. on my way to auction in Niles lots of comic
books. . That's my domain. Shaking it off.

It's a shame.

I feel that I hold the world in contempt.
There is no reward not for anyone.

True.

This week was the first week of ebay auctions. A business
direction proposed by me. The first two days I brought in nearly
two thousand dollars. Tomorrow I get a new computer a new
printer and the beginnings of an office. We have 3 part timers
who now take orders from me. The very direction that Wayne
movers is headed is one that I envisioned. Presented. And
received approval. I toured the southern united states on a three
week vacation.....I just can't believe that one of my forever failing
ventures has finally worked. And I forget that just this summer
that past I was homeless, in the woods outside Bremen. I have
changed my life.
It appears that at least around here when it comes to going
to an auction and analysing what we should buy and for what
price. That I am nearly the best. If not the best. And that is not
Braggadocio. The results speak for themselves. Wayne has been

going to auctions for years and never saw money like what we make every single auction.

There are lots of people more knowledgeable than me on a certain thing but it turns out maybe nobody is as knowledgeable about so many things as I am. And that is how we have become so dominant so quickly. It's maybe the greatest feeling in my life.

All this and sober too, right?

Nothing i do will ever be enough for you to just be happy for me. I have not messaged you much. Instantly i am reminded why..

I am happy for you—relieved.
But I have cycled through many of your excitements and enthusiasms—as have you. Several since January. I am not trying to bring you down, only to ascertain if sobriety might be a factor, in which case you are to be praised for that. And if it is not part of where you are now, it is something to be aware of. Don't give me any shit, please—I try to help—and do. I have helped your ex and the girls for years, steadily and reliably. So save your lip for some other customer.

I don't like to speak on my sobriety. The last time I tried to get sober when I relapsed I was tossed from my home and wife and the girls decided that I was a liar and beyond saving. Sobriety and addiction are my problems . I have a private life and those subjects are no longer ones of Wich I wish to speak..I gotta get back to work. Have a good night.

Thank you for that rationale. Do you have a steady address at the moment?

Fillmore road. Same place for a while now.

Do you still use a desktop. The house is moving along and I'm now considering office space. I have a limited budget and am having trouble making a decision Wich direction to go in. It has to handle lots of pictures and be able to print shipping labels and of course support several selling platforms, eBay Amazon FB Marketplace.

You need a printer and probably a Mac Pro Air.

A Mac pro air? Is that a desktop. It's cool to have a laptop but as far as managing things on the go I already have a phone.

Oh sorry. No, don't have a desktop any more.

I'm extremely nervous. I believe that I can make this into a viable business and so far I have delivered on every venture that I have proposed but online sales is competitive.

First two days I brought in nearly 2 thousand.. so very strong start. Ebay auctions are 7 days with the last day a flurry of activity....or potentially crickets... My stomach feels sour.
My mental picture of myself having an office one day always had a desktop. But I don't want to get dreamy about business.
Still the important thing. I'm about to have my own office!

Well lets just say I have a room with a computer that I want to call an office......

Then call it an office! You're the boss.

Hey... I need a favor. Ive screwed something up with PayPal . And I've got 100 dollars locked in the girls account. maybe we can talk. There must be a simple solution.

I don't know anything about PayPal really. Or how to get money from someone else's account...

Well I was on vacation and I wanted to send the girls some money. I asked if they had PayPal and they said yes. I assumed that since they are underage that you or Crystal had done it for them
Well they did it on their own and Crystal took it as personal offense that I sent them money. They say that they can not transfer money since they are minors. And the 100 dollars still sits in their avcount

Why do you need 100 bucks from her account?

Well I dont
Although i promised them 69 dollars for their first concert tickets. There was a portion of that towards that. It's a bit slow for me.. right now, to start up is going rough. Wayne leaves for OK tomorrow. Leaving me in charge of the 4 residential homes their occupants and everything else.
I'm going to try to fix it but if it can't get it figured out I wanted to see if you could pay some towards her concert tickets. But I'm pretty sure I've got it covered

I've just been a let down to the girls so many times.
When Wayne is gone I'm without a ride. But good news I see lawyer tomorrow

I'd rather not get involved in this—what concert, where, how late, with whom\ sorry.

Ok. I got it... Right I don't think along those terms. Your right. It's best not to get involved. Their mother can be so obtuse I'm trying to place you as an intermediary. Sorry. But I'm pretty sure this one is on the sunny side. I can't remember the concert. Jacob the performer or some shit. I am out of touch with familial morays.

Do you have an email address still?

Yea same.

I thought I'd send you an LL bean gift card that you could spend down on warm clothes etc. they would mail things to you.

That would be very nice. Thank you.

You should get an email with $500 on credit there; order over phone or online for home delivery. Let me know if any issues. See what you need there.

Happy Thanksgiving

I got the card thank you.

I hope you find things you need—they have more than clothes, but I figured you could use some good outerwear. Let me know if you have any problems. Enjoy the day.

Nothing is the same without Jason. Jason would have been with me every step of the way today as I built this electrolosis machine. For rust removal

What will you do with it? Remove rust I know. But business application? Must be one I suspect.

Vintage tools are the newest hot collectable. I've been cashing in. Well I don't know about cashing in. But I'm trying to get ahead. People just throw the tools out because they are covered in rust. sanding and scraping ruin the patina. While chemical removal can destroy the tool as well and often discolors the metal. This way is the best way. And it's cheap. I use an ac to DC converter and run pos to a sacrificial line of steel pieces to draw rust and run negative to the parts that will be losing the rust. Has to Be DC. alternating current continues to flip polarity. giving less than satisfactory results.

Enterprising!

It's one of the benefits of having me around. I'm a physics science guy. I've been staying sharp on that stuff my whole life. Finally making a difference in my life.
I brewed a chemical concoction to conceal burnt wire. By removing the oxidizing compounds giving our copper Bare bright status and top dollar returns.
I made a wire stripping Machine that strips wire bare with

mechanical efficiency. There were some fails but I'll keep those to myself.

I need some advice.

I'm here.

I found a funny looking blade covered in rust
After letting it sit for 24 in my electro rust remover I discovered that it was hand forged and potentially very old. I also found a Chinese mark near the tang. I suspect it was for butchering. But I thought it was cool. Others must agree I put it up at auction on a Facebook place and it's going for 85 dollars. With 3 hours left.

What did L.L. Bean say. They should refund the money. Somebody was spending down the card. They bought a belt not my size. Damn, did you know there is not an L. L. Bean in the whole state of Indiana. I looked

I called, They told me it was redeemed, once for another gift card, then again (by the second party) for another gift card. A scam operation. Do you know who got access to your number? Did you lose that phone?

No. I still have the phone.

They said there were no charges on it. No belt or anything.

Of course, erasing their tracks. Or they know I'd be waiting for the delivery in South Bend when it came.

In South Bend? So you do know who?

I don't know no, just an example. I don't think that kind of operation goes down here in Indiana but I really couldn't say.

They have names of the redeemers. But can't tell
me. They say nothing was ordered.

Names? No I don't have any names
If they have names why do they protect them.
You mean they have the name of the first guy who redeemed the card and they refuse to give it?

No criminal charges brought.

Why? How can that be? My shit was stolen from me How is that ok?

Then you bring charges.
I don't have the time. It was a bad idea.

I see.
I wont mention it again. Thank you for the card.

The photo You and mom and me.. do you think there is a different reality where we stayed a family? We look so happy. Life just gets fucked up.

I guess there are no sure bets in this world. We had something; it
slipped away. Maybe it's hiding somewhere.

I would like to think so. I had the same thing but it lifted like a fog and was no more.

When I was a kid I fantasized that this would happen even after she was gone. Who knew that it had already been.

Tomorrow. Phone. We try.

Ok

○○○○○

Christmas Eve 2021—that would be today—I have a phone message:

To hang up, press one, to prevent calls from this facility, press 9. I know what's coming. *Hello, this is a call from*—Josh (him: a voice and abjection I know)—*an inmate from the Saint Joseph County jail. To hear your payment options, press 0. To refuse this call hang up or press 1. To prevent calls from this facility, press 9. Your call was not accepted, please try again later.*

I have the "rap sheet" for this installment, visible on the jail's website. I printed it out: theft, resisting arrest, and a new one—false informing. $500 bond, on the "resisting law enforcement." There is his mug shot—sad, hangdog face, exhausted eyes at half-mast, looking into nothingness.

Calls me—once I manage to put money on my card for prison calls. Blah, blah, stole some food—from a UPS delivery truck. "I was starving, Dad." Caught on camera.

Nabbed. No defense but his hunger. His "boss," Wayne, wants nothing to do with him. Mentions, to me, drugs. Can I bond him out, he asks? Maybe the ministry can help him, he says. The 15-minute call ends.

I can't go on, not in this vein. Haven't I been here before, trying to extract a narrative out of chaos, a redemptive narrative out of incriminating chaos? A resolution, that is, on the narrative level; *story*, sneakily exonerating. It was from Joyce first, thanks to my third or fourth reading of *Ulysses*, that I learned that narrative resolutions in life were rare, that father and son do not recover themselves in each other, Bloom remains Bloom, the son of a suicide, and Stephen remains, for all intents and purposes, whatever that means, an orphan, a free radical flung beyond the reach and circle of his father, Simon, who does not approve of him (or much care for him). And despite the intervention of chance, i.e., the meeting between Bloom and Dedalus (in episode 9, Scylla & Charybdis)—with so much promise—it all comes to nothing (in "Ithaca"), Bloomsday ends in the early dawn of the day after Bloomsday, the two men have mugs of cocoa, take a leak together, and part, their respective lives go on. No, they end. No record do we have. (There's a book idea for you: *The Day after Bloomsday*.) All "true" resolutions are on the aesthetic level only, then; affirmation only in language— "*Yes*." Now I am learning the same thing from Beckett. He might've worn tight shoes to be "emulous" of his hero (father?) Joyce, as Deirdre Bair contends (though the odious "emulous" is Craig Raine's term), but Beckett didn't long believe in anything but separating from his father (hero?), his aesthetic working in the exact opposite direction, toward impotence (!) and failure and away from omnipotence. It is very sad somehow. Yet it is potency that brings the greatest sorrow, life then death.

And I find here the death of my first wife, in a dream, Josh's mother, Jason's mother, Damon's mother, of hypothermia on a cold rainy January night, at the edge of a lake, deep in the woods, having tried to walk home, with a bad cold, after a fight with her mother, with some drugs in her, with some beers in her purse, she left the boys at her mother's, to go home to her boyfriend, to a trailer I think, by the lake, in the woods, she was exhausted, she lay down in the freezing slush, took off her coat, balled it up for a pillow, just to rest, deeply cold enough to begin to feel warm, just to rest. By the Lake of the Woods, near Bremen, Indiana. A dream I find after reading Emily Dickinson poems.

> After great pain, a formal feeling comes –
> The Nerves sit ceremonious, like Tombs –
> The stiff Heart questions 'was it He, that bore,'
> And 'Yesterday, or Centuries before'?
>
> The Feet, mechanical, go round –
> A Wooden way
> Of Ground, or Air, or Ought –
> Regardless grown,
> A Quartz contentment, like a stone –

This is the Hour of Lead –
Remembered, if outlived,
As Freezing persons, recollect the Snow –
First – Chill – then Stupor – then the letting go –

A Quartz contentment. Jesus God where did Emily come
from?

And another, a dream, comes to me as Bob Dylan, in a small
bungalow he has rented in some small town, for a little
event, in the house, it is Bob's house, and with a handful of
people, including a handler or manager, Bob is performing,
he is strumming his guitar in a kind of living room, windows
behind him to a leafy street, streetlights like lemons through
the dark trees. It is evening. I am meant to accompany him.
I have a guitar though I don't play. Bob sings a verse, and
looks at me, a cue, a musician's cue. I am supposed to know
the song, not sure I do. I am meant to sing the second verse.
I say to Bob, "I can't sing." Bob moves on, not even a shake
of the head, a real pro. I try to strum along. I can't play
guitar at all.

Bob is mercurial. He is the Bob we have gleaned from all
his enigmas. He is self-absorbed. We are incidental. I am
incidental, an incidental, random accompanist. His mood
takes him outside. The handful of us wander out into the
town, we circle the town square after him, a soft evening,
Bob is strolling now, we stroll with him with no evident
purpose but to follow, to wander, to wonder.

We return to the house. Bob disappears through a door down some stairs off the kitchen, into perhaps a basement. I hear some voices, like some teenagers down there, maybe his children or grandchildren. A lean hound makes an attempt to nose out from the stairwell, curious at the goings on but the door is softly shut.

I wait at an island in the kitchen. I might still be needed. It is awful but it is my job for some reason. Then Bob is back, back in the living room with the windows behind him onto the leafy street, this is like the Hollywood hills as I imagine them, and Bob is preparing to resume. I better go to the bathroom.

I try the stairs to the basement. I hear the voices. The hound noses out as I open the door and looks at me but someone closes the door again. I head out toward a kind of vestibule. There is a cleaning woman tending to some chore and I ask her if there is a bathroom. She is Hispanic seeming. She nods toward a closet, a kind of utility closet with buckets and mops and there is indeed a toilet. I urinate there.

When I return, in case Bob expects me, or needs me, he seems to do neither. He has settled on the floor, he is despairing, he is crying, his face rumpled, his lower lip quivering. "Jesus wept," I think. Dylan weeps. He says abjectly, "Needless. I am so needless." His handler or manager looks at me. We are in a semicircle around Bob. We have no idea what to do. I wonder what "needless" could possibly mean. Is he without needs or unneeded?

∘ ∘ ∘ ∘ ∘

My son has another court date next week. I know it is his last. If he shows up. If he doesn't he's fled, somehow, or leapt to his death. Or built a fire on Main Street and shot it full of holes.

Has fled. He has fled the story at least, by virtue of his not leaving. His rap sheet—list of offenses and court dispositions and bonds and conditions—is now very long. He had not fled, he remains, because he cannot live on his own, in a county jail in Indiana, where he is poorly fed. He turned forty-five three weeks ago, forty-five years since he was born in the Hospital of St. James in Leeds, England. I send him a $25 care package each week ($25 is the maximum allowed; they don't want anyone turning into a purveyor to jail mates). He has refined what he wants in order to maximize the $25—they know the price of everything on the list of goods available from the Indiana County Package.com program, offering Drinks, Foods & Snacks, Health & Beauty, Clothing & Accessories. Although he could get a 3-pack of Andrew Scott boxers (white) for $9.60, or 3 Andrew Scott T-shirts (white) for $12.50 or a 15 oz. bottle of Elementz Coconut Lime Hair & Body Wash for as little as $1.90, he prefers 3 bags of Keefe Alturo Blend Coffee at $2.35 each, 10 ramen soups @ $.75 each, 2 8 oz. bags of Doritos at $2.60 each and cookies for whatever is left, whatever the cookie. By my math, $19.75 less the cookies, so $5.25 worth of whatever the cookie.

He, my son, Josh, has fled the narrative, as a death watch is not on the menu, drop down or otherwise.

But of course I must go on, as long as life persists, as it will, and this story will, in the presence of cowardice (mine, his) and wonder (same, I hope). And he goes on, you can't kill him. He's indestructible. Tomorrow is a special birthday, we are now in June, his twin daughters turn sixteen. Tomorrow, he stands before another judge. He expects time, prison time, moving from county lockup to state penitentiary. I will go for a visit in the fall, in that case, Michigan City, I hope, near his daughters, and be done with this by then as well. He tells me, as we pick our wounds, that when his jaw was broken and wired shut, he could hardly eat, and he could not do meth in his normal fashion (how?), so he had to shoot up, hence the syringe found in his latest arrest. Doing meth with a jaw wired shut. "It has healed perfect," he tells me. "They said it never would, my jaw would be all fucked up. But it healed perfect. I just want the metal bars removed but they won't do it." He told me: "They call it maxillomandibular fixation. Try saying that with your jaw wired shut. Comes out *maximama mama fix it*. Sort of."

Time to order a food package, ten soups, coffee, snacks.

○ ○ ○ ○ ○

The fields today, their sparse carpet of daisies as if threadbare still overwhelm with their eloquence, the sky a blue too deep for air, one could almost stir it like an open can of thick new paint, a circular splendor a thousand coats deep.

Come here now. My son. Come here now. Walk with me, through this field, under this sky. Now. Shade from this tree. Now. Be free. Walk, now.

In your mind from the third tier of the St. Joe County Jail, the one you leapt from—is that how you broke your jaw or were you beaten? Of course they beat you. Of course they beat you. Leap to here.

Come here now, time travel, let's talk magic. Let's talk soul not body, souls can fly. Come here now. The wolf and the lamb live together, led by a child.

I remember something like "ben paca" I would say to you, teaching you to walk, down on my knees, you waddled forth to me, "ven para aca" it is in Spanish, "come here," my arms outstretched, you grinning your brave grin, excited, at the step, at the steps, not even a diaper, little belly like a grapefruit, *ven para aca mi hijo*. Come here now. Come here now my son. *Ahora*.

I imagine correspondence.

I am right here motherfucker. You can't write me out of the narrative. I thought you knew better than that. You have tried, but you are what you write. Easier to write me out of your life, sure. You did. You gave me up. You gave me up to my mother. You signed papers no doubt. You wrote checks no doubt. And you ran, to other women, other partners, other families, anything to insulate you from me.

But I stayed still, didn't I. I got myself in trouble. I got myself in custody. Repeatedly. I needed custody all along, didn't you see that? I had to manufacture it. I had to orchestrate my own care, my own custody. And I got the cheapest kind of all: jail. You call it "carceral," don't you? That's a word you've learned in your circles, even though your father—my grandfather, whom I saw maybe twice, was a hack, a guard, a CO. Did grandpa ever say "carceral." Wasn't he called into Attica, with a hunting rifle? Yes, my father, I am in carceral custody. Cost me nothing, cost you nothing, and I can keep my eye on you. From here. My panopticon spot, I see all. I am the guard, you are the inmate. You would be happy tending from a distance to me from a distance, a thousand-mile corridor, no threat of me showing up, I'm in my chair, though you wrote that whole story about running away from me because "I" was free (a fiction). You even had me on the noble run from false suspicions I had tried to harm our Obama-man, I loved Obama, and you did too. But you made it so I was seen as a threat to him. Would you have turned me in, in that story, if I'd walked into that mountain cabin you kept as a retreat, even from your (latest) wife? You think I don't know Ibsen? You think I don't know what John Gabriel Borkman was about? Guilt and shame and misplaced male pride, that's what. You think I have it but that's what you have. Borkman was imprisoned by his wife in an upstairs bedroom. No such luck for you. Your women have been fooled by you, motherfucker. But you don't fool me. Yea I am stalking you, let's get it out there. You are safe when I am here, in some jail or another or prison in another state, about a third of the way across the country, almost another world. But Greyhound goes

133

right there, is at Port Authority now, I almost wrote "Poet" Authority. And I could show up and make my claim. "Papa!" You don't think I read this? I read it all. I know where you go, I salute you for it-an ingenious evasive plan, and must be interesting reading what you are reading while toying with these little high-flown theories of yours about bigtime artists that interest you who might be delicately searching for proof of filiation in the weeds of words. Nice. Keep looking in the weeds-sorry, the leaves!-for your children. But I'm not hidden or hiding. I'm here, Ben pa ca my ass.

Only a nightmare. But a nightmare, which speaks from somewhere. I write you back into the narrative.

○ ○ ○ ○ ○

You had your court date.
They cut you a break. Rather,
Gave you a chance: 4 charges dismissed, 6 years on the fifth one. But:

To be remanded to a Rehabilitation Diagnostic Center outside of Indianapolis to assignment to a state prison with a respectable rehab program. Successful yearlong residency will lead to a suspension of your sentence by the judge. At his discretion. Then halfway house till you are reintegrated into normal life and some kind of law-abiding independence. You have done this before. Your father picked you up at a halfway house in South Bend, out near the airport, along a strip of factories. He was surprised at your ponytail, wild grin, coiled athleticism. A prison vibe. Your hunger, scarfing fast food barely a breath while still in the drive-thru, burger and fries gone in ninety seconds. Then a smoke. A job was secured overnight, at a factory. Your father drove you there and picked you up. In six months you were back in.

I failed, you said. Always looking for the big lick, you said. Etc.

Bring honor back to your name, said your father who named you. Etc.

I will, you said. I will do that.

PART IV
The Magic

A now famous letter from Beckett, written in German, surfaced in Grove Press's *Disjecta*, an indispensable miscellany of Beckett's critical work, translated by Martin Esslin, and then was more canonically enshrined and translated again into English, by Viola Westbrook, in the first volume of the collected Beckett letters. It was written in July 1937 from Clare Street in Dublin, where Beckett holed up for a time in the offices of the family building firm. The letter was written to Axel Kaun, a German man six years junior to Beckett. They met early in Beckett's six-month retreat to Germany, introduced by a Hamburg bookseller.

The first reference to Kaun in the Beckett letters is to Mary Manning Howe, who had left Dublin (and Beckett) in August 1936 to return to Boston (and her husband) after their intense summer fling. Beckett tells Mary that Kaun is a "bookseller's improver," a rather arch description of someone who has just gotten a job at a large publishing house (Rowohlt) in Berlin. Shortly thereafter, the bookseller's improver was offering the young, unmoored Irishman a chance to translate a collection of German poetry. The unmoored Irishman gave it a meager try but did not really like the poet or the poetry, and declined—in the aforementioned letter, known now in Beckett scholarship as "The German Letter."

In the course of explaining to Kaun why he was writing to him in German and not English, and perhaps a little sheepish about turning down an opportunity to publish (and be paid for it) despite his lack of prospects, Beckett waded into assertions that have come to be, as the editors of the Beckett letters put it, "a touchstone in understanding SB's aesthetics."

To Kaun, 9 July 1937 (English translation by Viola Westbrook):

> "It is indeed getting more and more difficult, even pointless, for me to write in formal ["official" in Esslin, for the German offizielles] English. And more and more my language appears to me like a veil which one has to tear apart in order to get at those things (or the nothingness) lying behind it. Grammar and style! . . . It is to be hoped the time will come, thank God, in some circles it already has, when language is best used where it is most efficiently abused. Since we cannot dismiss it all at once, at least we do not want to leave anything undone that may contribute to its disrepute. To drill one hole after another into it until that which lurks behind, be it something or nothing, starts seeping through—I cannot imagine a higher goal for today's writer."

He goes on to praise Gertrude Stein for work that perhaps "come[s] closer to what I mean [where] the fabric of the language has at least become porous."

Beckett was thirty-one at the time. He had published a few things but had gained no real footing. A collection of ten stories, *More Pricks Than Kicks*, had found a publisher but few readers, selling about five hundred copies; his novel *Fair to Middling Women* was back in the drawer; *Murphy* was circulating in manuscript among publishing houses but attracting no interest. He was in a bad way, on the run from a promising academic career, from a scandalous sexual affair, from his overbearing mother, while still mourning the death of his father, who had died three years earlier. Whatever his six months in Germany, financed by his mother, was supposed to have done for him, it had done him little good.

But his wish, expressed so early in his career, if one could call it a career then, to drill holes in language in order to see what seeps through, is something that, though it evolved, never left him as a principal aesthetic goal. Beckett's work would range far beyond Stein-type logographs, into his poems, the "three novels," the other three novels, the nouvelles, all the plays for theater, radio, and television, and the prose works that concluded his writing life. Drilling holes in the language is a simple concept, easy to visualize, but in application over time, in Beckett's hands, it was sophisticated, variable, and often mysterious—a ruthless "dismantling [of] the regime of expression," in David Lloyd's elegant phrase. It was serious business to search for a "syntax of weakness" or to master an art of failure, to disrupt expectations at every turn, to use silence aggressively, to make an evening at the theater a hostile and threatening experience; to play upon the nerves and not upon the intellect with language unintelligible or assaulting or baffling. In doing so Beckett redefined what a novel could be and certainly what theater could be. The poetry too stands out as utterly unique—and totally Beckett: uncompromising in its reductions, its music both private yet unmistakable.

But let us ask, what seeped through the holes? Was it something or nothing, or both? Or neither? We know Beckett reveled in expressions of failure and demonstrations of how elusive were the foundations of being, for which he was always trying and failing to find a form. We know these things thanks to his writing about painting. In "Three Dialogues," mannered constructions between Beckett and *transition* editor Georges Duthuit, "B." says he prefers painting that is "the expression that there is nothing to express, nothing with which to express, nothing from which to express, together with the obligation to express"— another oft-quoted distillation of the Beckett aesthetic. He found the work of painter and friend Avigdor Arikha "fevering after the unself . . . the gaze beating against unseeable and unmakeable." He marveled at the work of Paul Cézanne because it was "incommensurate with all human experience whatsoever." These are among the famous Beckett articulations of his determination to find the "nothingness that seeps" through a practice that is broken apart. His own work teems with corollary examples, part of the canon—the aimless rituals in *Watt*, the sucking stone incident in *Molloy*, Krapp's drunken recollections of a past intimacy followed by a dismissal of it all, not to mention that mystery at the heart of *Godot* (has the world ended?), *Endgame* (has the world ended?), *Happy Days* (ditto), and the wintry prose texts of the final decade where isolation and want are rampant.

So: nothingness seeps through all right, we may presume with authorial zeal and intent. But nothingness is only half the story, half of what the young Beckett reckoned could result when one shot language full of holes. Might we look for the "something" that came through? And might we presume it has something to do with the search for a form to accommodate being? Or self? His being? Does language, properly abused, indeed allow "something" rather than "nothing" to seep through? Late in his life, Beckett told the theater director George Tabori, "While still 'young' I began to seek consolation in the thought that then if ever, i.e. now, the true words at last, from the mind in ruins. To this illusion I still cling." And of course in Beckett's final work, the poem "What Is the Word," he still sought the true word. And he seemed to glimpse it, or "the need to seem to glimpse."

This is where the terrain in Beckett studies gets tricky.

H. Porter Abbott, in his 1996 book *Beckett Writing Beckett*, presents a case for reading Beckett's work as autography. In doing so, he makes two remarkable assertions: that

Beckett is doing a kind of magic and that he is writing his self, whether consciously or not. It is just as remarkable that there have been no engagements in Beckett studies with the first, the magic, and few attempts to offer explanations as to what the last might look like—that is, what is the *self* that is coming through? Granted, in its simplicity it is a question that most any consumer of "Beckett" would ask: how does this relate to Beckett the person? And just as remarkably, Beckett scholarship, albeit busily historicizing Beckett, sorting out what he was reading, where he was, what manifestos he signed, what he believed in, never asks what of his self is in his works, this man who felt finding the form for Being was the challenge of art, who detected—and thereby acknowledged—in his study of Proust's *À la recherche du temps perdu*, the narrator's "resistance before the perpetual exfoliation of personality." Abbott does not venture a conclusion about the connections between work and inner life, what it is that might be beneath personality. And a scant few have expressed any interest in doing so. Dominic Walker is one of them. He argues that Beckett's anxiety about having emotionally hurt a former lover, Pamela Mitchell, is inscribed, literally, in *How It Is*, as "P.A.M.", the acronym for *pris les armes à la main* ("captured with weapons"), a widely used reference in the French press coverage of the Algerian war. Those designated as "P.A.M." were not prisoners of war, in the French government's logic, and therefore were unprotected from torture, as with the characters in *How It Is*. Walker's take is the rare antiformalist reading of a Beckett work. Another such approach concerns the anguish of Maddy Rooney in *All That Fall*. Both Beckett biographer Knowlson and seminal scholar Enoch Brater detect Beckett's feelings of bitter resentment in the text's assault on religion, which they speculate stemmed from Beckett's anger at the unjustified suffering of his recently deceased brother, Frank. Though these are the kinds of approach Abbott may be calling for, he reminds us that "Beckett always pulls us back to the questions of who speaks" and he attributes "the sustained originality of [the] work" to "self-writing or . . . autographical action." And, as said, to magic.

Abbott observes that in most Beckett works there is "an excess of invention." Even the simplest (seeming) or shorter works are never a one-note production. There are complexities of light and dark, sound and silence, figures obscured, revealed, taken away; figures that do not move. You have narrators being narrated, self being mocked, questioned, tortured, prepared for death. The questions Where now? Who now? When now? open *The Unnamable* and are never answered. Rather, there is bitter laughter. Whether in the longer plays, the small plays, the dramaticules; whether for stage, television, radio, or the page, there is one thing always—powerful, beautiful, lyrical writing overlayed with "such an insistent challenge to our capacity fully to grasp what it is we are seeing." Indeed, nothing is certain when "Beckett" is around.

I give Abbott great credit for hazarding this guess as to the "how." He employs the term "loops" to cover various strategies that work to disrupt the flow of narrative—citing the use of repetition, incantation, a backing up in order to leap farther ahead, like Pozzo's running start. Repetition indeed: the second act of *Godot* (the play where nothing

happens, twice, in Vivien Mercier's memorable phrase);
the repeat of the entire play in *Play*, the second half of the
abstract TV drama *Quad* repeated but in black-and-white
rather than color; Krapp repeating himself, listening again to
his identical testimony, skipping over parts, repeating parts.
Abbott says it plain: "Seeing the text as a representation of
conjuring gives a special license to its complex unreadability.
Our minds bent in the effort to grasp a fusion of stasis
and motion, past and present, word and action, we are
put through a cognitive warp, feeling in our synapses the
exquisite failure of generic expectations without which
magic does not happen." Abbott also cites the pacing in
Footfalls, the "gothic settings and arcane practices" that
pervade the later drama; and the disembodied voices, the
ghosts, the floating heads, the raps on the table in *Ohio
Impromptu*. He calls all these things "trappings of the
dark craft."

What Abbott is after is something to explain the enduring
power of Beckett's work generally. Why do these enigmatic,
fractured, obscure, abstract, contradictory, withholding,
violent, bitter, comic, confounding, formal, surreal, unreal,
too real, utterly bizarre and original works still get read and
performed and written about today around the world?

For me, the most powerful recurrent "loop," to use Porter
Abbott's term, is the appearance of children in nearly all the
major works, never in anything close to leading roles in any
of the texts, always tangential but weighted with mystery
and never easily dismissed. It is as if they are always there,

lurking inside the language and convention that Beckett is at pains to take apart always. As if they seep through.

Another Beckett scholar, Paul Lawley, in his (for me) foundational essay "Beckett's Relations," in the *Journal of Beckett Studies*, also grapples with the question of the repetitions in the work. In a section titled "Memories and Fragment," he references Stan Gontarski's claim that "the movement toward higher and higher levels of abstraction" in Beckett's work is "not so much to disguise autobiography as to displace and discount it." Although Lawley shies away from "the pursuit of biographical reference" and avows his intention to focus on the "recurring structures" that allow us to "recognize the nature and extent of the displacement," he cannot resist stating the obvious: "we cannot disavow our awareness that the fiction harbours memories." He adds, "We also know that the memories *traverse* the fictional texts, as though in a condition of alienation and banishment. They are insistent: they do not allow us to forget them." Such are the children in Beckett. The leaves *are* filled with children. The pages are.

Even so.

As I trust is evident by now, my interest in Beckett and childhood is a personal one, not a scholarly one. Likewise, my interest in Susan Howe is the same, born in a complicated way of my own life and its central attending concerns—the mystery of origins, the identification of family whether blood or not, and the responsibilities connected thereto. These concerns of mine have been mediated by my nearly lifelong interest in literary expression, and I must also admit that I have pursued these mysteries—of origin, of identification of family and responsibility—through my writing and my literary enthusiasms. Signature of all things I am here to read, mused Stephen Dedalus, and my confronting the work of Joyce and Beckett and, for a time, the American writer Harold Brodkey, has been motivated by a search for signatures pertinent to my own existence, identity, and development as well as my long struggle with a son of my own whom I did not raise but who is an unswerving yet endangered and endangering satellite to my adult life. Stories of fathers and sons and parents and children always open up passageways down which I walk, looking for recognizable figures and a kind of peace if not understanding.

Bloom and Dedalus continue to fascinate me—Bloom forever my senior, though I am now three decades older than Leopold, and Stephen forever my contemporary, even though I was only his age when I first wrestled with *Ulysses* nearly fifty years ago. So replete is that novel with what one scholar has identified as "structural latencies" that I am still treated to the discovery of latencies inherent in me as I process the text anew.

My earliest encounters with the work of Samuel Beckett were marked by bafflement and delight, unaccustomed as I was to the abstractions of his work, the eccentricity of the characters, their inaccessibility, and their doomed existence—more importantly, their awareness of the latter and their often comic, often bitter, resignation, all of it rendered in intricately constructed prose sentences, brilliant comic timing, and stunning invention.

Over the years, but especially in the last ten or so, I have come to understand that there are many layers in a Beckett work, some things deeply submerged, others misleading, many pointing to what is missing. The polymathic Irish genius seeds these works with deep, crucial recognitions of other great works, of literature, music, visual art, and, as has been proven in the current flowering of Beckett scholarship, his hitherto little-known multifaceted and profound engagement with history, politics, and justice. All these things make Beckett great company. As Moran, enraptured, said of his bees and their intricate flight patterns, "This is something I could study all my life and never understand."

○ ○ ○ ○ ○

I had known Susan Howe's work for many years, as one of my earliest literary enthusiasms was for the L=A=N=G=U=A=G=E school of American poets, entry to which I aspired to for a time. Though I have come to realize that Howe's work is too singular to be a true adherent to the doctrine of that school, she was recognized there as at least a fellow traveler, and her work and her reviews often appeared in L=A=N=G=U=A=G=E journals, for which we must be grateful. But when I got wind that she might be related to Beckett—indeed his daughter—my approach to her work and Beckett's changed. I soon found that it was no more than a rumor and it never became fodder for actual scholarship or literary or biographical analysis in either Howe's world or Beckett's. Still I could not, have not, let it go.

I have not thus far in this work grappled with the other hypothetical—that Beckett himself was aware of the uncertainty of paternity. He remained a good friend of Howe's mother and corresponded with Susan, though there are boxes of letters to both Susan and her mother and I assume their correspondence in turn with Beckett that remain closed without permission of Howe and her sister Fanny, also a writer. I have not ventured to ask for such, since my interest is only in what traces I think I can identify of that uncertainty, in both their respective oeuvres.

Searching for traces of any such uncertainty in the work of Beckett has been discouraging (if self-inflicted). Discouraging because it is not something that interests any other Beckett scholars and which even, at times, appears to be unwelcome. Still, if one narrows this interest down to the children in Beckett, there is no lack of brilliant scholarship, even if much of it seems conflicted and at times terribly wrong.

Certainly, Beckett's work is rife with children, and mysterious children, sometimes endangered, sometimes enchanted; at other times targets of hatred, aggression, even murderous intent within a piece, be it in a story or a play; and yet of course sometimes playing a key role in the work—the Boy in *Godot*, a messenger who works for Godot and delivers news of him; or the boy said to be wandering in the blasted landscape beyond the walls in *Endgame*; the "small boy" who appears for a climactic fifteen seconds in a recessed passageway in the television play *Ghost Trio*, dressed in a hooded oilskin "glistening with rain," who looks at the male figure and shakes his head disapprovingly, twice, before he turns and goes; "all the children walking in the dead leaves" in *Watt*; the orphaned girl in Kilkool; the young boy who is at the tragic center of *A Case in a Thousand*, who dies in a hospital bed; the child reported—by a boy—to have died under the wheels of a train in *All That Fall*; a boy and girl holding hands who approach Mercier in *Mercier and Camier*, greeting him with "Papa" only to be chased away by said father. And then the many seemingly autobiographical scenes of a young boy walking the Dublin hills with his father or the little boy who asks his mother a precocious question cruelly deemed impertinent, a scene replayed with variations in three different works. When combined with the countless instances of disgust at the sex act, at parturition, and at female genitalia, and the several coarse characterizations of women in general, the way is clear for Beckett scholarship to assert both misopedia and misogyny as consistent and troubling attitudes in the work.

This is disconcerting to any admirer of Beckett's work but it must be dealt with, and it is, in a variety of impressive sourcings of these attitudes in Beckett's supposed despair about life leading to suffering and meaningless death, and the derogatory judgments on women and children are to be thereby explicable, indeed unavoidable, positions on the matter. No births, no children, suffering over, or not commenced senselessly—the extremity of Schopenhauerian logic.

To characterize this as a logical creative consequence stemming from insight into human suffering, as if it were an inevitable end result of a brutal calculus, of course relieves us from attributing to Beckett a personal belief in these measures—it's philosophy not misanthropy. Swift didn't seriously believe that children should be eaten to bring an end to the Irish Famine, nor did the Beckett who cared so dearly for friends and family, and who was so moved by the human suffering, whether from illness, poverty, alcoholism, war, or heartless government, hold to these deplorable remedies to injustices pursuant to being born. There is nothing in his life that would suggest that. If he were childless, like Maddy and Dan Rooney in *All That Fall*, he nonetheless created works marked by the presence, or the absence, of children, whether in the family line or in the surround. In most works, you don't go very far before a child wanders in or enters a character's thoughts—or exits. Greeted without welcome often, but as often mourned or treated with tender solicitude or wonder. Children do seep through.

Although children, childhood, and family relations feature in nearly every major work and many of the smaller or lesser well known ones, and at times are central to what are considered autobiographically sourced episodes, they most often provide occasions of critical consternation or unease if they are not dismissed entirely by scholars.

Stephen Thompson in his *Journal of Beckett Studies* essay "It's Not My Fault, Sir: The Child, Presence and Stage Space in Beckett's Theatre," wonders "whether there is anything [at all] Beckettian about childhood in Beckett" as, in his view, childhood in the work "stands for simplicity, transparency, self-evidence." Of the character of the Boy in *Waiting for Godot*, who appears at the end of both Acts in the play, Thompson asks, "What is the Boy doing there at all?" and references Colin Duckworth questioning whether the Boy "is a character at all" as well as Regis Saldo's demotion of the Boy to "emploi de théâtre," a mere device. All this vaporizing of the Boy even though, unlike Vladimir, Estragon, Lucky, and Pozzo, he has apparent total agency, moves alone, comes and goes with purpose, has a sense of self, has a brother, an employer or master (Godot himself!); he even knows Vladimir by name ("Mr. Albert"), which Vladimir does not contest. As for the late prose piece *Company*, considered the most sustained presence of "the real Sam" or of "the real memories of the real Sam," Professor Daniela Caselli points out that Beckett's biographers (Bair, Cronin, Knowlson) either scoff at what they see as excessive sentimentality in the childhood memories or are discomfited by Beckett so indulging himself to the detriment of the modernist project. Caselli herself falls prey to a similar unease—"my contribution argues that *Company* questions the workings of authenticity and spontaneity implicit in the very concept of childhood."

Much of this scholarly thinking unfolds in the shadow of the critical attentions given in recent years to the notion of childhood by writers such as Jacqueline Rose, who makes the argument that children are immediately a knowable entity, without mystery, innocent, possessed only of a primary state of language, sexually free, and in all cases representative of its type—as a child—and yet bound up in all sorts of contradictions, which, in my view, leads to confused and overthought claims. Caselli glosses this scholarship in her omnibus review of three books in the journal *New Formation* concluding that childhood "is claimed to be absolute innocence and visionary knowledge, free sexuality and lack of sexuality, true originality and pure imitation." Somehow, children are constructs, not people.

It gets more tangled. Paul Stewart's undoubtedly pioneering book *Sex and Aesthetics in Samuel Beckett's Work* contains this observation: "The child is a figure of hate in Beckett's work." Terence Brown offers the stunning statement, "The Beckett universe is a curiously childless one." And in Kathryn Bond Stockton's *The Queer Child*, we have this door slammed on considerations of "the problem of the child as a general idea":

The child is precisely who we are not and, in fact, never were. It is the act of adults looking back. It is a ghostly, unreachable fancy, making us wonder: Given that we cannot know the contours of children, who they are to themselves, should we stop talking of children altogether? Should all talk of the child subside, beyond our critique of the bad effects of looking nostalgically in fantasy?

We "never were" children? I don't understand. Or want to. I was a child. It is forever internalized. I recognize myself in people (yes, people, not *emploi de theâtre*) who are children now. I see their wonder, their fear, the world of magic. I see the child my wife was, and is. It is magic but real. My son in a cage I see.

○ ○ ○ ○ ○

It was Daniela Caselli, from the dais of that MLA panel in New York in 2018, when I asked whether a personal brush with fatherhood might have affected Beckett's thoughts on abortion, which was the subject of her paper, who said to me, "I don't go there." It has been my experience in the wonderfully companionable community of Beckettians, from whom I suppose I now risk banishment, that they do not go there as well. This is understandable. An heir-to-the body would have been problematic for the Beckett Estate surely, and I have no reason to believe that there *was* such an issue. Still, the uncertainty that bedeviled Howe for years and Beckett—unless he was completely in the dark—is worthy of scholarly attention, if only to more soundly debunk the speculation.

"Doors open in May," Beckett wrote to Thomas MacGreevy in early March 1937 on word from Mary Manning Howe, who was huge with child. The doors would, in fact, not open until June 10, in Boston, for the birth of Susan Howe.

Mary Manning Howe left Belfast for Boston on August 22, 1936, on the *Caledonia*. Knowlson in his biography of Beckett reports, with Mary as his informant, that "They went out with each other regularly [that] summer. It was obvious that a sexual affair was going on and both of their mothers were frantic with worry. May Beckett called Susan Manning, saying, 'Please God when is she going home?'. . . In the first week of September," it seems Knowlson was told, "Molly, as she was known, took the boat back to Boston and everyone breathed a sigh of relief."

[Knowlson has acknowledged that he had the dates of the Belfast departure wrong and would correct it to August 22 should Bloomsbury reprint the biography.]

If the two Dublin lovers had a last farewell sexual encounter on, say August 20, then forty weeks or 280 days would make an estimated due date of May 27. Susan Howe, her first child, was born exactly two weeks late.

If the married couple, Mary and Mark DeWolfe Howe, had a reunion encounter upon her return on August 29, a strict forty weeks would bring a due date of June 5. So doing the math does little.

I can see one reason people "don't go there," as Daniela Caselli chose not to. It is not easy or in the least bit dignified to be musing about adulterous couplings and the births of children that might be troubling to any of the parties, especially in a literary study such as this. It is awful and shameful for me to do it. But I must own it.

All that concerns me here is the possibility that Irish-American artist and poet Susan Howe and Irish writer Samuel Beckett may both have developed their practices under the threat (or promise) of being daughter and father, and that their practices bear marks of the stress of not knowing beyond doubt something so crucial. They are extremely important artists. This would matter.

As I well know, uncertainty as to parentage can make one wonder, actively ignore, deny, fantasize, rue. It can make one fashion a certain physical look, as some believe Howe did, and as Beckett did early, styling himself like his literary father, Joyce. It can make one lose his or her self in genealogies of artistic, historic, or philosophical influence and pretension, as Howe and Beckett both do. As I have done—

My mother, my mother, whom I never knew, whom I never met, after a one-night stand in New York City with my father, my father, whom I never knew, whom I never met, gave birth to me at St. Vincent's Hospital and surrendered me on Armistice Day, 1954, to the Sisters of Mercy at the New York Foundling, who then entrusted me to the Coffeys, then of Poughkeepsie, New York. As she was dying of cancer in an upstairs bedroom in Rockville, Maryland, forty years later, my birth mother was heard to mutter, in a kind of delirium, "my little boy, my little boy," which puzzled all but the one sister who knew of me.

I had long wondered at the identity of both my mother and father. I suspected an unmarried nurse friend of my adoptive mother as my birth mother; or a neighbor who doted on me; perhaps one of my mother's unmarried sisters had given me over, or more fancifully, I could be the son of Jack Kerouac, given up for adoption in Greenwich Village by one of his girlfriends. Or perhaps I was the real product of the novelized affair in Thomas Gallagher's *Oona O'*, a book that I found remaindered in an Upper East Side shop, Oona with her "crazy thin legs" and rebellious spirit, who is left to contemplate raising a child on her own in New York City after an affair. It was Oona who gave me up. I wove many such scenarios from what I did know—that my mother had a beautiful singing voice and that my father was a "free-lance" writer. In the end I found that my mother had had a star turn in a Broadway musical and my father had written texts for Hallmark Cards, loved James Joyce, and ended up selling advertising for the *Philadelphia Daily News*. The fact that my mother's people (Bradleys) were from County Mayo and my father's (Gallaghers, no relation to Thomas the novelist) from Donegal made a different kind of sense of my attending Notre Dame, studying for a year in Dublin, and getting a master's degree in Anglo-Irish literature. Susan Howe talks about the telepathy of archives and poetry, but I would offer that even from the barest of information, however it is conveyed, one can divine if not a destination a path, a *how* to go if not a *where*. It has brought me here—the sun glistening the fields this morning in the Adirondacks as I work on another book.

∘∘∘∘∘

I once had a professor, in Dublin, at the School of Irish Studies in Ballsbridge, Professor Mays, formidably prenominated "J.C.C.," Oxford, Englishman, served in the

RAF. A handsome, tall, thin, angular man, very serious of bearing but with eyes that squinted with introspection and delight as he casually stood, his right foot slid to the left of his left, a precarious yet graceful perch, as of a heron. He walked us through *Ulysses* and Joyce's Dublin like a tour guide who is happy if you go off to explore on your own as long as you come back for a quiz or surprise essay question: "How much money did Stephen have at the end of the day?" or "*Perfume of embraces all him assailed*. If you agree that the syntax is 'Joycean,' explain why you think so." We were all astonished at his mix of gentleness and fierce intelligence— we understood that he was some kind of Coleridge scholar, but in Dublin, he was most actively involved in writings on Joyce, Beckett, and Brian Coffey. Like Beckett he was not enamored of the Celtic Revival poets or even those working with Irish history and political conflict, like Heaney, Mahon, the Longleys, Carson, Boland. He preferred the Continental Irish writers, the modernists—MacGreevy, Denis Devlin, Brian Coffey.

That was my junior year abroad. Graduated from Notre Dame the next year, I turned to Mays to recommend me to his Oxford College for graduate school (no chance) and, when I landed a slot at Leeds University, he suggested I write my thesis on Brian Coffey, and helpfully suggested an angle—a Thomist reading. Professor Mays thought there was work be done there. I wrote an awful thesis—Aquinas was way beyond me—but I graduated with near honors, a wife, and a newborn son. When I settled in the walk-up flat in Manhattan's Upper East Side and found an entry-level job in publishing, I was a long way from Dublin or Oxford or Leeds.

My marriage was going very badly, and fatherhood was a desperate struggle, while New York City beckoned with its degraded, bankrupt charms.

In the middle of the summer of '78 I receive a postcard from Professor Mays—

He is doing research in New York and suggests coming by for a visit. And he does; this elegant fellow in a nice linen suit arrives. He seems delighted to see me, to see us, Oralia with baby Joshua Brian, just a year old. I could use a haircut, I remember thinking. He makes himself comfortable on our makeshift, street-found furniture. Our top-floor apartment is airless, right under the baking tar roof; he takes a cold glass of homemade lemonade, and it is like the best thing he has ever had. There is something kind and fatherly about Professor Mays. He asks about the engineering magazine I toil at, my first job; I mention one of the other editors at work whose father he might know—William Barrett, the philosopher. I don't really know Barrett's daughter, but Professor Mays seems to approve of where I have landed. "He's very good," he says of the philosopher and author of *Irrational Man*. When he leaves, I find myself incredibly moved, that my Professor Mays is strolling along the blistering Manhattan sidewalk having visited me. He says he'd be taking a walk through Central Park to the Upper West Side. I wish I were going with him into the cool of the trees there.

I correspond with Professor Mays—Jim—over the years.

He says nice things about a few of my books and answers politely if economically to many queries I choose to bother him with, including probes about my interest in the Susan Howe connection to Beckett. It is Jim who mentions Mary Manning Howe's pronouncements in Dublin about *First Love*; he suggests I talk to Susan's sister Fanny. (I read her work; I don't.) He doesn't say much else, though he surprised me once by saying that Susan Howe "is a very good poet."

I pushed my Howe inquiries with others who were closer to the Beckett life and canon, and I did so, as we have seen, to little effect other than irritation. During visits to Dublin I had lunch a couple of times with Jim and his wife, Maryanne, at the National Gallery and, at his suggestion, the Chester Beatty Library. Pleasant meetings both, slightly bracing too, as, now older, Professor Mays is more abrupt and a little more impatient. Maryanne has to tend to things rather than have him negotiate the cafeteria-style offerings at each dining area. I do my best to help.

It is Jim who tells me of Conor and Judy Lovett, saying that they are "really very good. You must see Conor." Since then I have seen at least of dozen of their productions of Beckett work, and written about their company, Gare St Lazare Ireland. He also sent me back to MacGreevy, and to Coffey— his respect for them rekindling my earlier interests.

He spoke, too, with his cool passion, of Coleridge. I vowed to read him on Coleridge and took on his book about "The Rime of the Ancient Mariner," a poem we all know. Or I thought I knew.

His *Coleridge's Ancient Mariner*, from Palgrave (2016), promised to configure the poem as an experimental work that is central to understanding the Coleridge verse and prose *"and which has affinities with experimental work in the present."*

How was I to know or expect, given Jim's reticence, that the last three pages of the book would be about "a contemporary author whose work serves to reinforce and extend [a] point about writing that pursues a meaning beyond words"—which Professor Mays claims for Coleridge's work. "Poetry beyond the poem," he calls it. That contemporary author turns out to be Susan Howe.

Professor Mays writes that, like Wallace Stevens, Howe "explore[s] the echoes of a world beyond the day-world" and "hears dead voices of [the] Irish . . . Howe is interested in these voices at the edge of words for various personal reasons"—"her ancestors' history and in particular her mother's background in Ireland." He stresses the "eerie, haunted . . . [and] numinous" in Howe, "but most of all the Imaginary in the Coleridgean sense . . . leading to imaginary gardens with real ghosts in them." And (not unlike Beckett), Howe's "means to communicate such meanings" involve subtraction—"lines of print fragments of which only the top- or bottom-half of words are fully legible." It is a kind of magic she works, a conjuring, telepathy she calls it, like a séance with history.

In closing, as his Parthian shaft (I looked that one up—"a sharp telling remark made in departing"), Mays notices the fragments of his own edited *Poetical Works of Coleridge* in "the page area" of Howe's recent book *Tom Tit Tot*, and then in a flourish that ends his book and now ends mine, he quotes from *Waiting for Godot*:

> *To be dead is not enough for them.*
> *It is not sufficient.*
>
> *They make a noise like feathers.*
> *Like leaves.*
> *Like ashes.*
> *Like leaves.*

My son, now forty-six, has been transported to the Westville Correctional Facility. Today is my birthday. I am sixty-nine. He's in a rehab program. The sun is out. My son is in.

Petit Sot Poems

The motor moving inside the moving car (Gertrude Stein),
the rhythm inside the rhythm (Charlie Parker), in the heart
of the heart of the country (William Gass)—art's striving
for the part that represents the whole, *to whatever degree*.
Indices or abstracts, or as Beckett did at the very end of his
astonishing *Mercier and Camier*, a terse poetry summarizing
the two preceding chapters:

> *The life of afterlife.*
> *Camier alone.*
> *Mercier and Watt.*
> *Mercier, Camier and Watt.*
> *The last policeman.*
> *The last bar.*
> . . . .
> *Dark at its full.*

A precipitate or a distillate, then, two terms favored by
Beckett, not unlike the kind of thing Susan Howe produces,
in her poetic essay *Souls of the Labadie Tract*, depicting issues

of power and gender relations in Puritan New England by means of a scrap of fabric from Mrs. Jonathan Pierpont Edwards's wedding dress—all that remains of Sarah Edwards in the vast collection of the family's memorabilia held at Yale. The telepathy of *Her* archives as necessary, however spare the fact.

○ ○ ○ ○ ○

I brought myself to Argentina, to a conference on Beckett and poetry, me, too, looking for a precipitate, a scrap to hold and read; something to be told.

On the endless Avenida Corrientes, block after block of restaurants and bookshops, bookstalls, really—no front doors—and little kiosks on the sidewalk selling key chains, maps, and chewing gum, the sun blinding from the east in the morning and from the west in late afternoon. October, sun, and books everywhere.

On the second floor of the Centro Cultural de la Cooperación, in a small room seated with a couple dozen Beckett scholars, we are talking about the poetry of Samuel Beckett, here in Buenos Aires, where the history of repression and fascism has left a taste for the Irishman's work, the plays especially. I have made the long trip—my first since Covid broke out—to hear a friend, Jose Francisco Fernandez, talk about poems whose authorship is in dispute. These are the controversial "Petit Sot" poems, first mentioned in 1996 in James Knowlson's biography of Beckett, now detectable here and there as references in the four volumes of Beckett *Letters*—and increasingly the subject of scholarly essays.

Twenty-two poems in French, written in 1938, introduced to the world by Knowlson as poems that form "an independent cycle based . . . on the figure of 'Le Petit sot,' or Little Fool. The poems follow this little character, always in the first person, in a variety of guises, as horse rider, traveler, lion, moth, singer, searcher after the moon. . . . The poems re-create the games or fantasies of a little boy. They are simpler in vocabulary, syntax, and ideas than any of the other poems of Beckett at that time and look at first like stylistic exercises." Only one of them has been published, as a footnote to a letter to publisher George Reavey, cited by the editors of the Beckett letters:

> *je suis le petit sot*
> *il faut*
> *étre grand pour être malin*
> *et se tenir bien*
> *et faire comme eux*
> *et devenir heureux*

Not just another child in Beckett mysteriously appearing from the wings, speaking enigmatically if at all, but a boy, at the center, speaking in the first person. The lead, as it were, in the center ring, declaring, if this poem is of any evidence, the adorable aspiration to grow up, behave, conform, and thereby find *heureux*.

Beyond this, the poems were never published, and never, authoritatively, even attributed to any one author— puzzlingly, there is a camp that attributes the poems to Suzanne Deschevaux-Dumesnil, Beckett's partner and wife. There are no handwritten manuscripts (holographs) but for a single poem that seems in the series (for it mentions "petit sot"), handwritten, that turned up by accident in a gift of eleven volumes of Immanuel Kant from Beckett to his friend Avigdor Arikha in the 1950s. Over wine and oysters (I like to think) at La Closerie des Lilas, a favored haunt in Montparnasse, Arikha asked Beckett to sign the sheet of paper found in the Kant volumes and Beckett warmly obliged. We also have a set of texts, clearly typed on Beckett's typewriter—so say scholars—but again, with no supporting holograph or manuscript. These typed poems were found in the papers of the painter Bram van Velde with "Beckett?" scrawled on one page, as if in doubt. The same poems also turned up in a strange-looking typographic arrangement—side by side in ruled boxes—in the archives of Beckett's longtime French publisher Les Editions de Minuit, supplied by a composer who named Suzanne as the source, that is, the author—she was interested in the composer setting *her* poems to music, he said. According to this Minuit employee, Edith Fournier, a close friend of Suzanne's (and her literary executor), not only are these poems by Suzanne, but the ones in the van Velde collection, although typed by Sam, are also authored by Suzanne, who, Fournier reports, hated the typewriter, "la machine": Sam typed them for her, she contends. Fournier also claimed that the handwritten poem Beckett gave to Arikha, although inscribed and signed, is in fact in Suzanne's hand, not Sam's—it is Suzanne's poem, according to Fournier, Arikha is wrong, and his widow, Anne Atik, is wrong, and Knowlson and a string of others are wrong.

Although the official word is that Beckett scholars now have agreed to disagree on the matter, closer to the truth is that Beckett scholars agree that the poems are indeed by Beckett, but that position has been overrun by the proprietary interests of Les Editions de Minuit, with the consent of the Beckett Estate, which, while not supporting that the poems are by Suzanne, will not claim that they are by Sam either. Exile, then, for the poems of the Little Fool who fancied himself, among other things, the King. And for all we (can't possibly) know, may have matured, after the war, into *Godot*'s Lucky.

This accreditation dispute came to a rather ignominious end when the editors of the long-awaited *Collected Poems of Samuel Beckett* were forced to pull, at page-proof stage, the appendix containing an introduction to the poems as well as all the Petit Sot poems themselves. The fact that this requires us, or asks us, to believe that Beckett fraudulently promoted these poems as his own on several occasions—*or that Suzanne did*—does not seem to trouble the French house or the Beckett Estate or Edith Fournier.

Perhaps the poems are not good enough to inspire a decision—Minuit famously stood in the way of Beckett's first play being published, despite Beckett's explicit permission to Barney Rosset to do so—*Eleutheria* was a seventeen-character French farce, a far cry from the lean, austere

Beckett that arrived with *Godot* and became his signature style. For whatever the reasons—quality, questions of authorship—the "Petit Sot" remain orphaned, unclaimed, and unseen by anyone who has not visited the Beckett Archives in Reading, where copies of all these documents reside. Susan Howe might be more than right—history is hidden in the archives, waiting to be heard or seen. These poems I find as distillate to my long project.

○ ○ ○ ○ ○

Whether by Suzanne or Beckett, the Petit Sot poems were written in a year that would turn out to be propitious for Beckett, and by extension for Suzanne, a year in which, as Knowlson put it, Beckett found "a permanent home"— France, and to an extent, a home in the French language itself, and a place with a woman who would become his longtime partner.

Let's go there. The turn of the year into 1938 found Beckett living in a hotel in Paris, after a bitter quarrel with his mother in Dublin and a humiliating turn as a witness for the prosecution in a libel case against Buck Mulligan, aka Oliver St. John Gogarty, dealing with Gogarty's anti-Semitic slurs upon Beckett's beloved Sinclair relatives. Beckett was not that far removed from other trying times: eight months distant from his troubling sojourn in Nazi Germany, which he embarked upon as his scandalous affair with the married Mary Manning Howe flamed out. But the acceptance at last of *Murphy* for publication—and receipt of his first advance in late 1937, and a happy Christmas day spent with the Joyces in

Paris—augured well for the emotionally recovering Beckett. This bright upturn in his fortunes, however, abruptly darkened in January when he was stabbed in the chest by a stranger. Beckett nearly died, the blade just touching the pleura that covers the surface of the lungs. Among his many visitors—mother May, brother Frank, the Joyces, Brian Coffey, Peggy Guggenheim, and Nancy Cunard—was Suzanne, with whom he had had a casual acquaintance some ten years before. Recovering, his confidence boosted by the prospects for *Murphy* and now several other projects, Beckett began paying more attention to this intelligent, handsome, musically talented Parisian. Sam's "French girlfriend," Peggy Guggenheim called her, and though herself lately jilted by Beckett, Peggy lent them her car for a trip to Normandy.

Somewhere in there the Petit Sot poems were written by someone. Some two?

Sam and Suzanne found an apartment on Rue de Favorites. They would live there until they secretly married in Folkstone in 1961, after which they moved to Boulevard St. Jacques, their final Parisian residence.

○○○○○

The poems, as Jose Francisco said of them in his talk in Buenos Aires, quoting the great scholar John Pilling, "are childlike but not childish." Here, for all the silent, muted, bullied, insulted, despised, mysterious children in evidence in Beckett's works over the following half century of his

writing—from *Whoroscope, Godot, Endgame, Ghost Trio,*
All That Fall, Not I, Malone Dies, Molloy, The End, Company,
Watt, A Piece of Monologue, First Love, Murphy, Dream of Fair
to Middling Women, As the Story Was Told, Serena II, Film,
How It Is, Embers, Kilkool, A Case in a Thousand, Worstward
Ho!, Eleutheria, Enueg I, From an Abandoned Work, Texts for
Nothing, The Expelled, The End, That Time, The Calmative,
and *For Future Reference*, I count thirty-two works—is
something different, not silent but speaking, indeed holding
the floor in unabashed first person; not bullied at all, but
in full possession of a self; and rather than mysterious, the
Little Fool or, as I like to think of him, the Little Rascal, is
completely guileless, and convincing, as a voice of childhood
consciousness and being, and not a parody of it. It is speech
without irony, without fear no doubt, but with an appropriate
wariness that is wonderfully paired with the sunniness of a
happy childhood (as Beckett claimed he had—few believing),
angling for adventure and whimsy and perhaps, assuming a
bit of boyish even devilish derring-do, providing the author a
form of transitory respite. A way station, if you will, a happy
ride on a haywain in a summer harvest, as Europe darkened
in 1938 toward its nightmare.

And what was Beckett doing there, if he was there, in this
kind of regressive space, after thirty months of therapy
with Wilfred Bion, having survived that somehow, having
survived his mother somehow, now perhaps avoiding the
burden of being responsible for fathering a child, now
fatherless himself, now with a partner in Suzanne and a
little fresh traction in his writing? Was Beckett indulging

himself in childhood reveries (as opposed to memories)? Was he lolling about in the shoals of childhood fantasies? Was he learning to write in French, testing out the expressive potential of a severely limited vocabulary? Trying to write without style? Was he slumming privately, with Suzanne or not, in boyhood adventure? Was Suzanne channeling his boyhood for him?

It seems, *officially*, we don't know and we might never know. A universal theme—irrecoverable origins.

But if the Petit Sot poems were allowed into print, readers could see for themselves the unmistakable Beckett style, tiny tautologies revolved and explored with economy; tender, intimate depictions of the simplest of things of the kind that dot even his mature work.

ooooo

The story of the Petit Sot poems doesn't quite end here. There is a coda to this coda, about yet another incarnation of the texts that circulated, however narrowly, the details as known laid out by Jose Francisco's original research, that would ask us to believe yet another instance of willful misrepresentation on Beckett's part, if we are to credit the idea that Suzanne was their author.

Jose has determined that Erika Tophoven, translating partner to Beckett's German translator, her husband Elmar, found thirteen poems tucked inside the inaugural issue of *Evergreen Review* (1956), copies of which Beckett had thanked Barney Rosset for sending him. The issue contained ten poems by Beckett from the 1930s along with his short story "Dante and the Lobster." Erika surmised to Jose that Beckett sent these Petit Sot poems to Elmar because a German prisoner, Karl Franz Lembke, an enthusiastic reader for *Waiting for Godot*, had managed to stage fifteen performances of the play with a prison troupe and written a letter to Beckett that moved Beckett deeply ("this was our Godot," wrote Lembke). Beckett wanted to help the man. He asked his German publisher to give Lembke 200 deutsche marks out of his royalty account and asked Elmar to pursue having Lembke translate the thirteen simplest poems from the Petit Sot group, to which Beckett claimed he would be adding more poems. Lembke, granted a measure of freedom due to the acclaim for his *Godot*, was allowed to meet Elmar, in a café in Frankfurt, but no money or poems changed hands, after which Lembke disappeared, never to be heard from again. On the run.

There is no evidence that Beckett sent the Tophovens the other nine poems. They exist only in the Bram van Velde papers, and in the jettisoned page proofs kept in the Beckett Archive in Reading. But Erika Tophoven's testimony is unequivocal that Beckett's expressed intent was to provide the additional poems, *his to provide*. How could these Petit Sot poems not be Beckett's? Still, a long note now dying, another question sounding out and unanswered, as in the Charles Ives composition, New Haven, 1906, "The Unanswered Question." Or sounding here, to end on a Beckettian note:

From *Worstward Ho*, one of his last works:

Nothing to show a child and yet a child. A man and yet a man. Old and yet old. . . . One bowed back yet an old man's. The other yet a child's. A small child's.

Or as in Howe, from *The Liberties*, an early work near contemporaneous with Beckett's above:

Do not come down the ladder

ifor I

haveaten

it a

way

Or here:

Some children write their own endings, theirs to write; fathers do not but in times of tragedy—not now yet, no. My son in the woods with a handgun. My son, in a trembling shade.

Central Park, 1978. Courtesy of Michael Quinlin